THE SEVENTH AMENDMENT

AN ILLUSTRATED HISTORY

ROBERT J. MCWHIRTER

Published in the United States by Constitution Press
an imprint of RR&G Enterprises LLC
PO Box 26666
Tempe Arizona 85285

Originally published in the United States as a chapter of
*Bills, Quills, and Stills; An Annotated, Illustrated,
and Illuminated History of the Bill of Rights*.

Distributed in the United States by Applewood Books
1 River Road
Carlisle, MA 01741
toll free: 800-277-5312
main: 781-271-0055

For bulk purchases for associations and other large groups,
please contact Applewood Books.

Library of Congress Control Number: 2017958120

ISBN: 978-1-945682-07-0

Design and layout of text by Quadrum Solutions

THE SEVENTH AMENDMENT

The Seventh Amendment

"In Suits at common law, where the value in controversy shall exceed twenty dollars, the right of trial by jury shall be preserved, and no fact tried by a jury, shall be otherwise re-examined in any Court of the United States, than according to the rules of the common law."

—The Seventh Amendment

The Declaration of Independence indicted King George III because he deprived us of *"trial **by** jury."*[1] The Seventh Amendment for civil cases, *"preserves"* *"the right of trial **by** jury"* if the parties are arguing about more than twenty bucks.[2] The Constitution at Article III, Section 2, mandates that *"Trials of all Crimes . . . shall be **by** jury"* and the Sixth Amendment orders that *"[i]n all criminal prosecutions"* trial shall be *"**by** an impartial jury . . . ."*

In the generation before the Constitution, the influential judge, Sir William Blackstone, extolled *"trial **by** jury"*:

> *The trial by jury ever has been, and I trust ever will be, looked upon as the glory of the English law.*[3]

All of these pronouncements of *"trial **by** jury"* assume another choice.

There once was.

---

1. THE DECLARATION OF INDEPENDENCE para. 20 (U.S. 1776).

2. "Dollar" comes from the Low German "*taler*," which was a large silver coin from the sixteenth century. JOHN AYTO, DICTIONARY OF WORD ORIGINS 179 (1990). A "dollar" in colonial New England referred to the Spanish "piece of eight." Anyone could make change with that soft silver coin by cutting it in as many as eight parts. Hence our term "two bits" refers to a quarter (i.e., two bits of the piece of eight). The Continental Congress on July 6, 1785, adopted the "dollar" for U.S. currency on  Gouverneur Morris and Thomas Jefferson's suggestion because the term was widely known but not British. Calling a dollar a "buck" is for "buckskin," referring to the price for a male deer hide. *Id.* at 82.

3.  3 BLACKSTONE, COMMENTARIES ON THE LAWS OF ENGLAND 379 (Univ. of Chicago Press 1979) (1765–69). Also, "[t]he trial by jury . . . is also the trial by the peers of every Englishman, which as the grand bulwark of his liberties, is secured to him by the great charter." *Id.* at 342–43. As mentioned in

William Blackstone

other chapters, Sir William Blackstone (1723–80) was an English judge and professor who wrote COMMENTARIES ON THE LAWS OF ENGLAND, a historical and analytic treatise on the common law published from 1765 to 1769. It was extraordinarily influential in both England and colonial America and remains an important historical source on the common law. *See,* for example, Julian S. Waterman, *Thomas Jefferson and Blackstone's Commentaries,* 27 ILL. L. REV. 629 (1932–33), and for a brief discussion of Blackstone as a basis for the Seventh Amendment, see Steve Bachmann, *Starting Again with the Mayflower . . . England's Civil War and America's Bill of Rights,* 20 QUINNIPIAC L. REV. 194, 250–51 (2001).

Blackstone knew of a time when the defendant had other choices for trial: compurgation, ordeal, or battle.[1] "*Trial by jury*" was a later addition that, over time, won out. But "*trial by jury*" owes something to the tradition of compurgation, ordeal, and battle, which were, after all, open and adversarial.[2] And like modern trials they often made for good entertainment.[3]

WHEN A TRIAL REALLY *WAS* A TRIAL: COMPURGATION, ORDEAL, AND BATTLE

Although we can hope that today's trials are more just, they are not nearly as much fun as the old types, at least for the spectators.[4] The main forms during medieval times were compurgation, ordeal, and battle. Given that the period of their use spans over one thousand years, the exact modes and manner of each varied. For most of the Middle Ages both church and secular courts used procedures we would recognize, though in a very primitive form: private accusation led to an open trial by compurgation ("*purgatio canonica*"), ordeal ("*purgatio vulgaris*"), or combat (which was actually another form of trial by ordeal or *purgatio vulgaris*).[5]

---

1. *United States v. Singer*, 380 U.S. 24, 27–28 (1965):

> *At its inception [trial by jury] was an alternative to one of the older methods of proof—trial by compurgation, ordeal or battle . . . Soon after the thirteenth century trial by jury had become the principle institution for criminal cases . . . yet, even after the older procedures of compurgation, ordeal and battle had passed into disuse, the defendant technically retained the right to be tried by one of them.*

Today the parties can choose a trial before a judge–a "bench" trial–but only after they formally waive trial by jury. See Fed. R. Crim. P. 23.

2. *See generally* James B. Thayer, *The Older Modes of Trial*, 5 Harv. L. Rev. 45 (1891–92).

Trial by Jury program (1875)

Scene from *Trial by Jury* (1875)

3. From light comedy to heavy drama, the jury is the platform.

Gilbert and Sullivan's comic opera *Trial by Jury* (1875) was a Victorian hit subjecting the legal system to satire.

Trial by Jury (Morgan Creek 1994) was a thriller/drama about a blackmailed juror during a mafia trial. *The Juror* (Sony 1996) had a similar premise and story line.

As for television, the jury appears countless times as a plot device or character. *Law & Order* usually ended with the jury. The *Law & Order* franchise's third spin-off was *Law & Order: Trial by Jury* (March 3, 2005– May 6, 2006), focusing on criminal trials in New York City.

Perry Mason, of course, never won his cases from the jury because his cross-examination left no doubt, much less a reasonable doubt, as to the defendant's innocence.

However, for real drama nothing beats the classic 12 Angry Men (United Artists 1957). Henry Fonda and a cast of the best character actors of the day are riveting. Based on a very good stage play, 12 Angry Men was remade for television with a very good cast and adding a greater racial dynamic among the jurors. 12 Angry Men (MGM Television 1997). Though a good production, it will always be compared to the 1957 Fonda classic. An interesting script change would be to include women on the jury, but that is left for an enterprising screenwriter.

The classic 12 Angry Men (United Artists 1957)

4. But for sheer spectacle, it is hard to beat the O.J. Simpson farce.

O.J. Simpson in the famous white bronco with his police tail driving in formation

5. "*Purgatio*"—In English we get "purgation" or "purge." Just as a modern trial is to "clear one's name," the purgative effect of a medieval trial was to "clear one's soul."

Dante between purgatory and Florence by di Michelino (1465)

Thus these trials were closely related to the notion of purgatory, or clearing one's soul as part of the ultimate trial of final judgement. Dante's *Divine Comedy* is but one literary illustration.

These trials were accusatorial with a known complainant or plaintiff and open confrontation.[6] The inquisitorial procedure of medieval Roman and continental law (the "*ius commune*") was accusatorial and presumed the accuser's innocence.[7] All these modes of trial were part of an accusatory trial tradition, reflected in the religious and cultural notions of the person's final trial and judgment before God.[8] Our Anglo-American trial by jury is the heir of this tradition.

COMPURGATION, OTHERWISE KNOWN AS WAGER OF LAW OR TRIAL BY OATH

During most of the medieval period, compurgation was the main accusatorial procedure.[9] If a defendant could swear his innocence and produce the required number of "compurgators" or "oath helpers" to swear they believed the defendant's oath, he would win his civil suit or, if a criminal trial, his acquittal.[10] The English also called it "*wager of law*" because the "wage" was the defendant's promise or oath.[11]

---

6. A hanging and an early English illustration of trial by combat, an open and accusatorial mode of trial. *See* J.H. Baker, An Introduction to English Legal History 5–6 (4th ed. 2002) (regarding the older forms of trial).

Ma'at wearing feather of truth

7. Walter Ullmann, *Some Medieval Principles of Criminal Procedure*, 59 Juridical Rev. 1, 4 (1947), *reprinted in* Walter Ullmann, Jurisprudence in the Middle Ages (1980); Anthony Morano, *A Reexamination of the Development of the Reasonable Doubt Rule*, 55 B.U. L. Rev. 507, 509 (1975) (arguing the presumption of innocence, a mainstay of modern criminal trial procedure, comes from canon law and Roman law).

Day of Judgment by Memling (1467–71)

9. Compurgation trials were important in the history of the right to remain silent. *See* **The Fifth Amendment, an illustrated history**, in this series, Constitution Press, 2017.

10. George Jarvis Thompson, *The Development of the Anglo-American Judicial System: History of the English Court to the Judicature Acts*, 17 Cornell L.Q. 9, 16–17 (1932). *See generally* R.H. Helmholz, *Crime, Compurgation and the Courts of the Medieval Church*, 1 Law & Hist. Rev. 1 (1983).

11. Black's Law Dictionary 1416 (5th ed. 1979). "Wager" has the same Germanic root ("*wathjam*" or "pledge") as "gage" and "engage," all of which preserve the original notion of "giving a pledge or security." It is also the root of "wedding." Ayto at 564.

The chip or marker symbolizes the wager or promise to pay

8. Examining a last judgment scene reveals the elements of a modern criminal trial: a judge = Christ; a bailiff = Saint Michael; a half-way house = purgatory; souls huddled for judgment = a chain gang; a Department of Corrections = hell; souls on a scale = defendants in the trial courtroom; the graves = pretrial detention; pleading souls = sentencing allocution; angels pulling at the soul = public defenders; demons pulling the other way = prosecutors. (A prosecutor might be inclined to switch the last two.)

Christianity did not invent this idea of a last judgment. In Egypt, the goddess Ma'at measured out justice for the dead in the Hall of Two Truths. Ammit, a horrid hybrid of cat, crocodile, and hippopotamus, placed the hearts of the dead on a pan and dropped a feather of truth on the other. If the feather sank the scale, the departed gained entrance into the Kingdom of the Dead. But if it rose, outweighed by the heart's burden of deceit, Ammit would eat it, abandoning the owner to oblivion. Sadakat Kadri, The Trial: A History, from Socrates to O.J. Simpson xvii (2005).

The origins of the compurgation trials in England are Anglo-Saxon. Originally, the compurgators were probably the kinsmen of the accused or party.[1] Justice was communal; its enforcement involved clan and family relationships. It was this communitarian nature of justice that made the system work.

In small communities a false defendant would have a hard time rounding up eleven neighbors as oath helpers.[2] Rough justice prevailed; even an innocent defendant who was a jerk would have a hard time finding oath helpers, and perhaps that was the point.

Not just fear of damnation from perjury assured justice in compurgation trials, but also the process itself.[3] Obviously, though, damnation for breaking an oath had a lot more power in medieval society than in ours. If the accused could not get the required number of compurgators, he could elect to have trial by battle or ordeal.[4]

Different times and different types of cases required various numbers of compurgators. Eventually, however, the generally required number became twelve oaths, the defendant and his eleven oath helpers.[5] This shows compurgation trials as a basis for our modern twelve-member jury.

The word "compurgator" is synonymous with "conjuror" and "juror."[6]

The thing to remember with compurgation is that the oath *is* the evidence.[7] Today the oath is just part of the jury's credibility determination.

TRIAL BY ORDEAL– GOING THROUGH FIRE AND WATER:

We tend to view trial by ordeal as nothing more than primitive superstition contrasted with our supposed enlightenment.[8] This misses the point: the ordeal was about mercy!

From what we can glean from the records, a defendant had

---

1. Thayer, *Modes of Trial*, at 58.

2. R.C. Van Caenegem, The Birth of the English Common Law 66 (1988); Frederick G. Kempin, Jr., Historical Introduction to Anglo-American Law 49 (3d ed. 1990); Baker at 74.
    An example of this was Queen Uta of Germany, accused of adultery in 899 and acquitted only after eighty-two knights confirmed her chastity. Kadri at 20.

3. Dante puts the great traitors, or oath breakers, in hell's very heart. Brutus, Cassius, and Judas get munched on for eternity by Satan, the greatest oath breaker of all.

4. Helene E. Schwartz, *Demythologizing the Historic Role of the Grand Jury*, 10 Am. Crim. L. Rev. 701, 707 (1972).

5. Van Caenegem at 66; Kempin at 49.

6. Kadri at 20.

The Conjurer by Hieronymus Bosch (sixteenth century) Note the character on the left stealing a money purse

    The synonym "conjuror" has come into modern English to refer to someone who performs magic tricks to amuse or trick an audience, that is, a magician. The original meaning from "conjuration" (from Latin "*conjure*," "*conjurare*," or to "swear together") can mean an invocation or evocation (the latter in the sense of binding by a vow). The original Latin, "*conjuration*" or "*conjurison*," formerly meant "conspiracy." Webster's New Int'l Dictionary 565 (2d ed. 1942).

7. The same is true for the other modes of trial of ordeal and battle. These supernatural proofs and the oaths upon which they rested were absolute proof. Baker at 72.

8. See Thayer, *Modes of Trial*, at 63–64 ("*scholars discover it [the ordeal] everywhere among barbarous people . . .*").

9. "*Its actual effect was to save many people, about whom there was little human doubt of their guilt, from capital punishment and maiming.*" Margaret H. Kerr, Richard D. Forsyth & Michael J. Plyley, *Cold Water and Hot Iron: Trial by Ordeal in England*, 22 J. Interdisciplinary Hist. 573, 594 (1992). *See also* Pollock at 295 (noting high acquittal rate).

King William II

10. Kerr at 580 ("*The majority of people who underwent the ordeal passed and saved their lives.*"). *See also* Kerr at 578, 579, 581 tbl., and 586 (for examples and statistics).

a 68 percent success rate at ordeal.[9] Most people who faced ordeal passed.[10]

This is why the English kings saw it as a limitation of their authority, as the second Norman King, William II (William Rufus) commented:

"What is that? Is God a just judge? Damn whoever thinks it! He will answer for this by my good judgment and not by God's—which can be folded this way and that as anyone wants it."[11]

The kings didn't like the church's control. But the "withering of ordeal" was not judgment by God— God already knew if you were guilty! Rather it

was remitting the case *ad iudicium Dei* ("to the judgment of God").[12] As contemporary writers noted, the ordeal is a form of "grace" (we would say "commutation") for the guilty.[13] God could give you an earthly pardon, and the ordeal was your purge, not necessarily a trial of the facts.[14] In England, the Assize of Clarendon in 1166 specified that defendants would face the ordeal after a presentment jury, the precursor to our modern grand jury, had already determined guilt ("*malecrditus*").[15]

Ordeals involved elaborate rituals allowing all manner

of subjectivity.[16] In England the two main methods were of hot iron and water:

- **Hot iron:** In this ordeal, usually for women, the accused grabbed an iron bar, which a priest had blessed, and walked a certain number of paces.[17] Her hand was bandaged and three days later a "jury" unwrapped it to see if the wound was infected. If not, she was absolved.

- **Cold water:** In this ordeal, usually for men (unless the charge was witchcraft), a priest blessed a pool, making it holy water. The accused was tossed in tied up.[18]

---

14. *Quoted in* Peter Brown, *Society and the Supernatural: A Medieval Change*, 104 Daedalus 133, 140 (1975). *See also* Kerr at 575 (stating the quote as "*What is this? God is a just judge? May he perish who henceforth believes that.*"). William was responding to the acquittal of fifty men for violating the forest laws. This quote also reflects the emerging church/state power struggle. Later Henry II would order an acquitted defendant from the ordeal to "adjure" the realm (i.e., banishment) but not forfeiture of his goods. Pollack at 180.

15. Brown at 138. Sir Frederick Pollock, *The King's Peace in the Middle Ages*, 13 Harv. L. Rev. 177, 295 (1900) notes that the ordeal was originally an appeal to the local pagan god of water or fire.

16. Van Caenegem at 69. Rebecca V. Colman, *Reason and Unreason in Early Medieval Law*, 4 J. Interdisciplinary Hist. 571, 582 and n.34 (1974) (clergy generally conducted ordeal trials).

17. Baker at 72.

18. Roger D. Groot, *The Jury of Presentment before 1215*, 26 Am. J. Legal Hist. 1, 3 (1992). The ordeal was especially useful when the jury was unsure—"*leave it to God.*" See Kerr at 577.

Modern grand juries find probable cause, and our trial or petit juries then find the defendant not guilty or guilty on the higher standard of proof beyond a reasonable doubt. This two-stage process came from the Middle Ages. In Europe, a form of inquest ("*inquisitio generalis*") developed to determine whether a *prima facie* case existed against the accused followed by the actual trial either by compurgation or inquisition ("*inquisitio specialis*"). *See* Ullmann, *Medieval Principles*, at 18. In England, the presentment jury developed from the inquest to send the case first to compurgation, or later ordeal, or later to jury trial. R.H. Helmholz, *The Early History of the Grand Jury and the Canon Law*, 50 U. Chi. L. Rev. 613 (1983) (arguing canon law as the source of our modern grand jury).

1. "*God might be believed to speak in an ordeal, but the human group took an unconscionably long time letting Him get a word in edgewise.*" Brown at 137. *See also* John W. Baldwin, *The Intellectual Preparation for the Canon of 1215 against Ordeals*, 36 Speculum 613, 629 (1961) (noting examples of the subjectivity in ordeal).

If the point was to really leave it all up to God, then why not just use dice or a coin to decide the question? *See* Fisher at 600–01.

2. *See* A.K.R. Kiralfy, Potter's Historical Introduction to English Law, 4th ed. 353 (1958). *See also* description in Kempin at 59–60; Van Caenegem at 65.

See the illustration of a widow taking the ordeal for her dead husband by grasping a bar of red-hot iron. The bar does not burn her, thus proving his innocence.

3. Kadri at 27. *See also generally* Danny Danziger & John Gillingham, 1215: The Year of Magna Carta 183–85 (2003); Van Caenegem at 64–65.

Ordeal of water

If he sank he was absolved because the holy water accepted him—or, conversely, the water repels the sin. They then fished him out (presumably before he drowned). The ordeal of cold water was akin to a rebaptism, where the soul came out of the water purged of sin.

It was the church, not the king, that controlled the process. If the defendant faced the king's justice, it most surely meant hanging or maiming. Thus it was much better to face an ordeal and the chance of God's "grace."[1] And a look at the procedures in detail shows how the defendant might get that grace.[2]

The ordeal of hot iron, for instance, involved a mass where the priest put the iron in the fire "*and sprinkle[d] it with holy water*" (of unspecified amount and temperature). After the priest took the iron out of the fire, he was to lay it on wood. (The wood absorbed some of the heat.) Then the priest was to read the Gospels (of unspecified length and reading speed) and then again "*sprinkle holy water over the iron*" (again, of unspecified amount or temperature). The accused then took the iron and carried it for "*nine paces*." (No mention of how fast the accused was to walk or, for that matter, run.)[3] Even at this point a few good calluses could assure God's mercy.[4] Then the priest or official bandaged the hand (unspecified as to how or with what) and waited three days, when the priest or a jury would decide if the wound had healed

---

1. Kerr at 573–74 asserts that the ordeal's mandatory use was only from the Assize of Clarendon in 1166 to the Fourth Lateran Council of 1215. Even Kerr, however, notes that the ordeal was mentioned "*in a number of [much earlier] Anglo-Saxon codes.*" Id.

3. See Kerr at 588 (describing the ritual).

2. Other ordeals. Several other types of ordeals existed in Europe at different times.

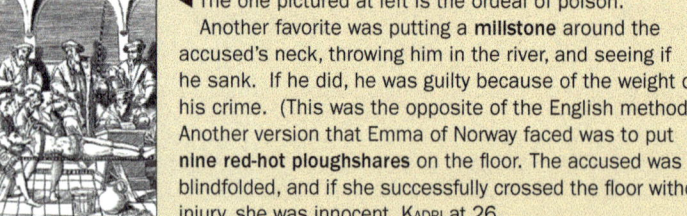

◄ The one pictured at left is the ordeal of poison.

Another favorite was putting a **millstone** around the accused's neck, throwing him in the river, and seeing if he sank. If he did, he was guilty because of the weight of his crime. (This was the opposite of the English method.) Another version that Emma of Norway faced was to put **nine red-hot ploughshares** on the floor. The accused was blindfolded, and if she successfully crossed the floor without injury, she was innocent. KADRI at 26.

For others, usually clergy, there was the ordeal of a **coarse morsel** of bread. If, after fasting for a number of days, the accused choked, he was guilty.

An early form, called the **cauldron ordeal**, was to have the accused reach in a pot of boiling water for stones. If after a time the hand became infected, the accused was guilty.

In the **ordeal of bier**, the accused touched the victim's body and was condemned if the corpse bled anew. Id. at 37. Thus, in the trial of ordeal there was an early form of Crime Scene Investigation (CSI) with the belief that the dead could tell you who did it.

Edward the Confessor's mother, Emma of Norway, walked on nine red-hot ploughshares to prove she did not commit adultery with the Bishop of Winchester

---

4. Don't forget the Leidenfrost effect! See Kerr at 590. This is what causes water drops to skip off the frying pan's surface instead of immediately turning to steam. The heat causes the underside of the water drop to vaporize, making a buffer and the bounce.

Johann Gottlob Leidenfrost first described this effect in 1756.

◄ Modern Fijian fire walkers do not get burned because of this effect.
The holy water on the iron plus the accused's own perspiring palms would have given protection.

5. Brown at 139; Kerr at 594.

6. Kerr at 594 (noting modern studies show that infection before the fifth day is uncommon in burn cases).

7. Why not? There is no need to be cynical about everything! "*Ego te absolvo*" ("I give you absolution") is the statement a priest makes upon giving absolution-or, updated, "*You beat the rap!*"

Michelangelo's God on the Sistine ceiling

"normally."[5] If yes, that was the end of the ordeal.

Thus, in the ordeal of hot iron, the accused had at least four chances for success:

- the iron caused no injury because it was allowed to cool;

- the accused may have had a second- or third-degree burn, which would not have shown up as an infection on the third day;

- the bandage was sterile and no infection developed;[6] or

- God spoke and worked a miracle.[7]

All in all, it was a lenient test.[8]

The ordeal of cold water had similar subjectivities. In the tuck position, a person who expels air will likely sink and thus pass the ordeal.[9] Also, women did not usually face the ordeal of cold water. Their higher body fat would have caused them to float and thus fail.[10]

The available records show a pass rate of 82 percent.[11]

Women did face the ordeal of water in one class of cases: witch trials.[12] These trials killed 60,000 to 100,000 people over two centuries.[13] *"Swimming a witch"* became the trial norm for witchcraft persecutions.[14] Out of fear and superstition Europe relaxed criminal procedure to get after these servants of the devil.[15] But witch trials were a subversion of the normal process of mercy.[16] In the same way its modern equivalents subvert justice.[17]

---

8. Kerr at 593 (*"It would appear, therefore, that if the presence of infection on the third day after the ordeal was the test of guilt, it was a very lenient one."*).

9. Kerr at 587 (noting scientific studies showing that after maximum exhalation the floating rate falls to almost 0 percent in males over age fifteen).

10. Kerr at 582–83, 586–88. A "Rubenesque" woman would not have stood a chance in the ordeal of cold water!

Venus at the Mirror by Rubens

Swimming a witch in Bedford. Sahe later hanged on March 30, 1613.

11. Kerr at 588.

12. English women were nine times more likely than men to be charged with witchcraft and twice as likely to be hanged. Kadri at 116.

Witchcraft defendant in the tucked position

13. Kadri at 105.

15. The Catholic Church originally taught that even believing in witches was a sin. Saint Augustine in the fifth century reasoned that only God could do magic and thus it was *"an error of the pagans"* to believe that *"some divine power other than the one God"* could do anything magical. Kadri at 106. Then after five centuries of teaching that it was blasphemous to believe in witchcraft, the church declared it a hearsay to deny witches existed. *Id.* at 109. But in places where the church was strong, the witch persecutions were both less frequent and milder. *Id.* at 111.

16. Without a strong central government or church, Germany was particularly bad. But in England, because of grand juries and petit juries, fewer than one in four defendants went to the gallows, a number far less than in any other country in Europe. Kadri at 117. *"Satan always got far less bang for his buck in England."* *Id.* at 118.

Saint Augustine

17. Senator Joseph McCarthy and **Roy Cohn** at the McCarthy hearings' modern witch hunt for communists.

Arthur Miller's play THE CRUCIBLE (1953), ostensibly about the Salem witch trials, was really about McCarthyism.

14. The idea was that because witches partook of Satan's ethereal essence, they were unnaturally light and bobbed to the surface. Kadri at 112. This is the same reason they can fly on a broom.

This lead to the belief that water killed witches, which is why the Wicked Witch of the West melts in THE WIZARD OF OZ when Dorothy dumps water on her.

In a more satirical turn, Sir Bedevere from MONTY PYTHON AND THE HOLY GRAIL (Fox Video 1975) summed up the reasoning of witch trials: *"Witches burn, and so does wood, so witches are made of wood; wood floats on water, and so do ducks, therefore, if she weighs as much as a duck, she is a witch."*

The Wicked Witch of the West

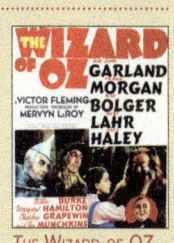

THE WIZARD OF OZ (MGM 1939)

But even if the accused failed the ordeal, the church's mercy could still extend to prevent hanging. The defendant could often take refuge in the church and buy his life by selling his freedom, that is, becoming a slave.[1] The kings resisted the practice. With the Assize of Clarendon of 1166, Henry II banished those who passed the ordeal, and denied the ordeal to those who confessed or those a presentment jury found to be of ill repute and who had taken stolen property.[2]

Henry II and the other English kings had several reasons for opposing ordeals. One, of course, was power. The kings wanted control over the church's jurisdiction. In addition the nature of justice was changing from private to public. The king had a role now in dispensing his justice and, as the source of justice, collected hefty fines in the process.

The church too moved away from ordeals as a way of resolving disputes. The church had always called the ordeal the "vulgar" mode of trial ("purgatio vulgaris"). Stories abounded of innocent people hanged after ordeals. Voices in the church warned that the ordeal immorally *"tempted God."*[3] Finally in 1215, with the Fourth Lateran Council, the church prohibited clergy from participating in ordeals, a restriction that effectively ended the practice.[4]

The ending of ordeal trials left an open niche in English criminal procedure. The church courts continued to use compurgation but, in the expanding king's courts, juries replaced ordeal.[5] Thus the Fourth Lateran Council of 1215 had more to do with the growth of jury trials in England than *Magna Carta* of the same year.[6]

1. Kerr at 589 n.30.

2. The term is *"adjournment of the realm."* Kerr at 575, 578 n.10; VAN CAENEGEM at 69–70; Groot, *Presentment*, at 22–23.
   The Assize of Clarendon prohibited those accused of serious crime from purging (ordeal or compurgation) and required them to leave England within forty days. BLACK's at 110. Clarendon began the transformation of English law from divinely ordained systems of trial by ordeal or battle toward what we now call the "evidentiary" model, beginning the common-law trial by jury.

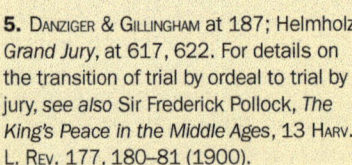

King Henry II

3. Baldwin at 628–29 (recounting the many voices in the church on the immorality of ordeals). Men were studying both law and theology in the church's universities at this time, undermining belief in the ordeal. DANZIGER & GILLINGHAM at 186. See also Brown at 136; VAN CAENEGEM at 68–69.

4. Specifically, Canon 18, on ordeals. Baldwin at 613; KADRI at 35, 50.

5. DANZIGER & GILLINGHAM at 187; Helmholz, *Grand Jury*, at 617, 622. For details on the transition of trial by ordeal to trial by jury, see also Sir Frederick Pollock, *The King's Peace in the Middle Ages*, 13 HARV. L. REV. 177, 180–81 (1900).

6. Fisher at n.20 (citing Roger D Groot, *The Early Thirteenth Century Criminal Jury*, in TWELVE GOOD MEN AND TRUE: THE CRIMINAL TRIAL JURY IN ENGLAND, 1200–1800, at 3 (J.S. Cockburn & Thomas A. Green eds., 1988)); see also Pollack at 180.
   For a detailed analysis of ordeal procedure and its place in medieval society, see generally Trisha Olson, *Of Enchantment: The Passing of the Ordeals and the Rise of the Jury Trial*, 50 SYRACUSE L. REV. 109 (2000).

7. Daniel Klerman, *Settlement and the Decline of Private Prosecution in Thirteenth-Century England*, 19 LAW & HIST. REV. 1, 11 (2001).

8. Thayer, *Modes of Trial*, at 45, 65–66; VAN CAENEGEM at 80; Pollock at 295. Actually, the source of trial by battle is subject to considerable scholarly debate. See, for example, Baldwin at 621, noting the source as the Lombards, VAN CAENEGEM at 65, noting the scholarship showing the Franks as the origin, and KIRALFY at 348, noting the relation to the Saxon blood feud. The Normans themselves may have gotten the custom from their own Scandinavian roots. Norsemen used the *"holmgång"* (or *"holmganga"*), a death duel, to settle disputes.

9. Because a person facing wager of battle was usually a knight, he had a squire to act as his "second," to arrange the details of the ceremony with the opposing squire. But see PRINCE VALIANT (20th Century Fox 1954), were Valiant fought trial by battle even though he was still the squire of Sir Gawain. Often the squires could resolve the disputes beforehand, eliminating the need for the combat. Henry II's reforms in the Assize of Clarendon in 1166 encouraged trial by jury and legal ways to avoid the wager of battle. This is one story of why lawyers even today use the title "esquire" after their names. This engaging story, though, is probably pure fiction. See H.W. FOWLER, A DICTIONARY OF MODERN ENGLISH

The Holmgång by Johannes Flintoe

TRIAL BY BATTLE, OTHERWISE KNOWN AS TRIAL BY COMBAT, JUDICIAL DUEL, WAGER OF BATTLE, TRIAL BY HIS BODY

No trial is more adversarial, confrontational, or open than trial by battle. Originally, the participants were the parties, and thus the term "*trial by his body*."[7]

Trial by battle probably came to England with the Norman Conquest.[8] It was a judicially sanctioned duel among nobles because only nobles, generally Normans, could bear arms.[9] Thus, even after the conquest, trial by battle never seemed to gain much currency among the Anglo-Saxons, and it became the Norman (French) mode of trial.[10]

The Normans, though, did sanction trial by battle for Anglo-Saxons

"[i]f a Frenchman shall charge an Englishman with perjury, or murder or theft or homicide or [robbery], the Englishman may defend himself, as he shall prefer, either by the ordeal of hot iron or by wager of battle. But if the Englishman be infirm, let him find another who will take his place." [11]

A "Frenchman" had the option of acquitting himself *"by a valid oath*." Later the person challenged would decide whether to have battle or jury.[12]

As time passed the law allowed a "*witness*" to stand in for some parties—in other words, a champion. Thus the English term for the procedure was "*wager of battel*," from the oath or "wager" of the witness-champion.[13]

Originally, champions fought for women, the young, old, or sick.[14] The witness-champion was to speak from his own knowledge or that "*of his father*" and would thus defend his testimony. Before battle, the two champions would swear to the truth of what they said.[15]

Usage 167 (2d ed. 1965) (noting that the term was just adopted by barristers but not solicitors in England, but that today could

Don Quixote and Sancho Panza by Pablo Picasso

be had by any adult male).
But the most famous squire of all time is Sancho Panza, Don Quixote's sidekick. "*Panza*" means "belly" in Spanish.

10. Thayer, *Modes of Trial*, at 66.

THE 13TH WARRIOR (Touchstone Pictures 1999) has a version of a *holmgång*. The movie and book are roughly

based on BEOWULF, with the movie's Viking leader called Buliwyf, with lines such as "*Luck, often enough, will save a man, if his courage hold*," a paraphrase of "*Often, for un-daunted courage, fate spares the man it has not already marked*." *See* SEAMUS HEANEY, BEOWULF: A NEW VERSE TRANSLATION 39 (2000).

11. Laws of William ch. 6, *quoted in* George C. Thomas, III, *History's Lesson for the Right to Counsel*, 2004 U. ILL. L. REV. 543, 562 n.139 (2004).

Don Quixote and Sancho Panza by Gustave Doré (1863)

12. BELLAMY at 36. *See* Roger D. Groot, *The Jury in Private Criminal Prosecutions before 1215*, 27 AM. J. LEGAL HIST. 116–25 (1983) (on how the appellee (i.e., the one challenged) could avoid trial by battle).

14. DANZIGER & GILLINGHAM at 181; Groot, *Prosecutions*, at 116.
What to do with women was always a problem. A woman could offer to prove the appeal "*as the court adjudges*." Kler-man, *Settlement* at 11. The non–battle worthy or women were usually put to the ordeals of cold water or hot iron to prove innocence. *Id.* at 12.

IVANHOE (MGM 1952) had actor Robert Taylor's Ivanhoe fighting as the champion of Elizabeth Taylor's Rebecca. Rebecca is in love with Ivanhoe but he goes for Joan Fontaine's Lady Rowena instead (not the choice I would have made, but there it is!). The film is an adaptation of Sir Walter Scott's IVANHOE (1819).
But as this medieval drawing shows, women could fight with the male opponent handicapped in some way.

Classic Comics version of IVANHOE

15. Thayer, *Modes of Trial*, at 68.

13. *See* BLACK'S at 1416. As with compurgation the oath was the evidence. KADRI at 20.

The witness-champions swearing their oaths before battle

Trial by battle was often used in land disputes, providing the basis for claiming that the "champion" would actually know who had the right claim. This allowed the champion to be a compurgator, or oath helper. In fact, compurgation trials eventually replaced trial by battle in most cases.[1]

In England it was supposed to be illegal to hire a champion. By 1275, however, the requirement (actually by then a legal fiction) that the champion be a witness was dropped.[2]

This practice of having champions was handy for English kings. It would have been unseemly as well as impractical for the king to have to fight in every dispute or, indeed, every time a crown official charged someone with a crime. Thus the king had his own champion.[3]

Fundamentally, trial by battle was another form of ordeal based on the notion that God would only let right prevail, *iudicium Dei*.[4] But the church discouraged the practice even more than other types of ordeals.[5] Such contests were expensive and thus unfair to the poor, most of whom had no training in the use of arms.[6]

Moreover, the church was adopting a more rational means of dispute resolution.[7] Trial by battle, as with other ordeals, tempted God by asking

---

1. Baldwin at 616–17.

2. Thayer, *Modes of Trial*, at 68. DANNY & GILLINGHAM at 181 (regarding the practiced of having "champions").

3. The champion of the King of England rode into Westminster Hall at the king's coronation, challenging "*if any person shall deny the king's title to the crown, he is to defend it!*" The Dymoke family has held this office since 1377. WEBSTER'S NEW INT'L DICTIONARY 447 (2d ed. 1942).

The king's champion figures into the Arthurian legend. *See* EXCALIBUR (Warner Brothers 1981) and CAMELOT (Warner Brothers 1967). It is also central to the movie EL CID (Allied Artists 1961), about the Spanish national hero El Cid Campeador, meaning "the king's champion" against the Moors in Spain.

In CAMELOT, Guinevere needed a champion because the king, Arthur, sat as judge over the court and thus could not defend her.

Julie Andrews and Richard Barton in the 1960 play CAMELOT

Charlton Heston, in his pre-NRA days, thinking "*swords don't kill people, people kill people.*"

Heston champions gun rights.

4. The biblical story of David and Goliath formed the agrument for the procedure. Baldwin at 618. *See*

1 *Samuel* 17 describing how David killed the giant Goliath with a stone from his sling. Some medieval theologians compared trial by battle to the just war theory. Baldwin at 623.

David and Goliath by Caravaggio (1600)

5. Baldwin at 613.

Theologians argued the precedent of Constantine's prohibition of gladiatorial contests. *Id.* at 614 n.10.

Pollice Verso by Jean-Léon Gérôme (1872)

6. Thayer, *Modes of Trial*, at 67 n.1 (noting Saint Louis abolished the practice as unfair to the poor).

In England, however, the great monasteries were often involved in land disputes and thus had to retain champions. KEMPIN at 56.

7. In the late eleventh century, the church and European lawyers rediscovered Justinian's DIGEST, which showed that the Romans had differentiated between proof and verdict. KADRI at 49.

8. Baldwin at 618, 620, 628 (citing to the arguments of Saint Augustine). Still though,

trial by battle made for great spectacle.

9. William Shakespeare's *Richard II* has an example of trial by combat between Bolingbroke and Mowbray. But the combat ends up not being to the death when Richard banishes both parties. See KORNSTEIN, SHAKESPEARE'S LEGAL APPEAL 202–06 (1994). For the actual historical account, see Peter Earle, *Richard II, in* THE LIVES OF THE KINGS AND QUEENS OF ENGLAND 85 (Antonia Fraser ed., 1975); see also KURT VON S. KYNELL, SAXON AND

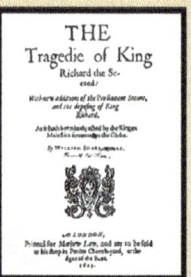

THE
Tragedie of King
Richard the Se-
cond.

acceptance of something other than God's rational world.[8] Indeed, when selecting a champion, the parties hardly put full faith in God—no one picked the biggest wimp.[9]

In 1215, the church's Fourth Lateran Council also prohibited clergy from participation in trial by battle, which discouraged the procedure. Other modes of trial took over, such as compurgation. As time passed the inquest in ecclesiastical courts and European kingdoms replaced battle and the other ordeals. In England it was trial by jury.[10]

The emerging concept of the "king's peace" added to the demise of trial by battle.[11] In criminal cases the new king's courts extended and protected the king's peace by alleging that the defendant did a crime "wickedly and in felony against the peace of our lord the king." Because the king is now the accuser-as is still seen in the caption of criminal cases in Great Britain as Rex (or Regina) v. The Accused-the defendant cannot seek trial by battle "since the king fights not, nor has none other champion than the country."[12]

The English, however, did not formally abolish wager of battle until 1818.[13] Some, however, argue the practice continued throughout the nineteenth and even twentieth centuries in the duel code.[14]

MEDIEVAL ANTECEDENTS OF THE ENGLISH COMMON LAW 161 (2000).
See MONTY PYTHON AND THE HOLY GRAIL (1975), which has a version of trial by combat with the Black Knight getting his arms and legs cut off but famously yelling "Okay, so we will call it a draw!"

Both IVANHOE and MONTY PYTHON AND THE HOLY GRAIL were filmed on location at Doune Castle in Scotland. Since 2004 the castle hosts its annual Monty Python Day.

10. Baldwin 614; Thayer, Modes of Trial, at 67. See also Groot, Presentment, at 1, 24 (on the origins of the adversarial system from juries). Regarding the jury as substitute for trial by battle, ordeal, wager of law (compurgation), and inquisitorial procedures, see Morano at 509 and BARBARA J. SHAPIRO, "BEYOND REASONABLE DOUBT" AND "PROBABLE CAUSE" 3 (1991). For the view that early common-law trials had much in common with inquisitorial procedures, see Landsman II and Langbein, noting that up until the late eighteenth century trials were inquisitorial. See also Amalia D. Kessler, Our Inquisitorial Tradition: Equity Procedure, Due Process, and the Search for an Alternative to the Adversarial, 90 CORNELL L. REV. 1181 (2005) (noting the American tradition).

11. See The Sixth Amendment from this series, Constitution Press, 2017.

12. Pollack at 179–80.

13. In 1818, a party threw a gauntlet into the Court of King's Bench, causing the court to rule that the system was abolished. BAKER at 74, n.12, citing Ashford v. Thornton, (1818) 1 B. & Ald. 405; Stat. 59 Geo. III, c. 46. In 1984 a Scottish defendant tried to wage battle, arguing that the 1818 rule only applied to England. Id. See also Alison L. LaCroix, To Gain the Whole World and Lose His Own Soul: Nineteenth Centruy American Dueling as Public Law and Private Code, 33 HOFSTRA L. REV. 501 (2004) (arguing that the duel code ("code duelo") came from trial by battle); Ellen E. Sward, A History of the Civil Trial in the United States, 51 U. KAN. L. REV. 347, 353 (2003) (noting that the duel was a "vestage" of trial by combat).

14. See ROBERT BALDICK, THE DUEL: A HISTORY (1965).
The Burr-Hamilton duel is the most famous in American history. The men meet at Weehawken, New Jersey, where the dueling laws were more lenient, hoping their duel would revive their respective political fortunes. Instead it ended Burr's political future and Hamilton's life. For the code duello, see the very good movie THE DUELISTS (Paramount Pictures 1977), Ridley Scott's first feature film, starring Keith Carradine and Harvey Keitel. Regarding defendants' attempts to assert the code duello as a defense in homicide cases, see Griffin v. State, 274 S.W. 611 (1925), and Ward v. Commonwealth, 116 S.W. 786 (1909).

Perhaps the longevity of trial by battle is due to the ideal it embodied: an open confrontation of two champions fighting for what is *right*. What courtroom lawyer sees him or herself in any other way?[1] And before we scoff at the notion that God will protect the *right*, don't we still believe in *iudicium Dei*? Name a classic Western where *right* does not win![2]

TO PLEAD OR NOT TO PLEAD-THAT WAS THE QUESTION

In the days of ordeal, battle, and compurgation the defendant could often choose not only his mode of trial but also his court: king, church, or local lord's. The accused needed to plead, in a sense accept jurisdiction, to start the case. Over time the effect of the Fourth Lateran Council was to leave but one form of trial: the jury.[3]

This raised a theological problem: having a party or defendant submit "*to God's judgment*" was allowed (after all, every soul would face it sooner or later), but, to the medieval mind, it was improper to require a person to submit to any form of *human* judgment (after all, people still had free will).[4] Specifically, medieval English courts could not bring themselves to compel a prisoner to "*put himself on the county*," that is, submit to trial by jury.[5]

The problem then became how to get the accused to accept—that is, to "plead to," *de bono et malo* ("for good or ill")—the jury. If the accused pleaded "*not guilty*," the judge would ask, "*How will you be tried?*" Answering the question meant that the accused accepted the court's jurisdiction and would not be pleading "*upon his clergy*."

---

1. Consider, for example, **Clarence Darrow** and **William Jennings Bryan** during the 1925 *Scopes* trial.
    The movie and play INHERIT THE WIND (United Artists 1960) is a fictionalized account of the Scopes Monkey trial. The title comes from the King James Bible, *Proverbs* 11:29: "*He that troubleth his own house shall inherit the wind: and the fool shall be servant to the wise.*"

2. From HIGH NOON (United Artists 1952) to TOMBSTONE (Hollywood Pictures 1993) to STAR WARS (20th Century Fox 1977), the theme is *iudicium Dei: right will triumph!*
    In the trial by battle, right wins, then ▼

and now. ▼ (Okay, so it's really "*A long, long time ago, in a galaxy far, far away,*" but you get the point!)

3. BAKER at 508. *Also* DANZIGER & GILLINGHAM at 189; KIRALFY at 247; KEMPIN at 63–64; Fisher at 588–89.

4. Pollock at 181–82.

5. From ordeal trials to jury see Pollack at 181; Klerman, *Settlement,* at 12.

6. BAKER at 508; BLACK's at 621 (noting that the question would have been "*by God [an ordeal trial] or country [a jury trial]*"). See also COLIN R. LOVELL, ENGLISH CONSTITUTIONAL AND LEGAL HISTORY 149 (1962).

7. This is the origin in some jurisdictions of the rule that a defendant has thirty-five peremptory challenges, the thirty-sixth constituting a refusal to plead. BAKER at 508 n.42.

8. See Pollack at 181–82.

9. BAKER at 508 (citing an act of Parliament in 1275). *See also* Anthony Musson, *Twelve Good Men and True? The Character of Early Fourteenth-Century Juries,* 15 LAW & HIST. REV. 115, 134 (1997) (noting the procedure of a starvation diet to get the accused to submit to trial by jury).

If the accused was a lord he would answer *"by God and my peers,"* which meant, up until 1948, he would get a trial in the House of Lords. If he was a commoner he pleaded *"by God and my country"* or *"by God and the country"* or to *"put himself on the country,"* meaning trial by jury.[6] *"Country"* meant the petit jury of twelve. The clerk would respond, *"God send you a good deliverance,"* a throwback to the older modes of trial of *iudicium Dei*.

If the accused would not plead, either by silence or by rejecting the customary three jury panels of twelve, he had *"refused the common law"* (*"tanquam refutans legem commune"*).[7] This created a problem because without the prisoner's submission, the procedure could not go forward, though the refusal to submit was an independent offense of contempt against the king's power, that is, contempt of court.[8] All a judge or sherriff could do was put him in jail, a *prison forte et dure*, meaning under harsh conditions and meager diet, to force the accused to plead.[9]

Prison forte et dure, however, eventually took a deadlier turn, becoming *peine forte et dure*, a procedure where they pressed the accused under heavy weights until he pleaded or died.[10] Thus, when a defendant refused to plead and stood mute, he went to a *"press room"* until he submitted or suffocated.[11]

The reason some defendants endured pressing was because if they died before trial they died innocent and thus saved their estates.[12]

The simple expedient of entering a plea for the defendant eluded the common law until 1772, when Parliament made a mute plea the equivalent of a guilty plea.[13]

---

10. Baker at 508–09. Andrea McKenzie, *"This Death Some Strong and Stout Hearted Man Doth Choose": The Practice of Peine Forte et Dure in Seventeen- and Eighteenth-Century England*, 23 Law & Hist. Rev. 279, 283 (2005).

11. *See* Levy at 233.
 Peine forte et dure is not the same as **execution by crushing**, which occurred after conviction. In ancient times, the Carthaginians executed people this way, and for over four thousand years of recorded history it was common in South and Southeast Asia using elephants. *Le Tour du Monde* by Rousselet (1868)

12. If convicted the king got the condemned's property (i.e., it was *"escheated"* to the crown), leaving the defendant's heirs nothing. Mckenzie at 289 and n.12. Regarding bravado and class issues with jurors of a higher powered class, see *id.* at 304.
 After Henry VIII, pleading in religious trials became very important. In 1586 Saint Margaret Clitherow refused to plead to the charge of harboring Catholic priests. She did this to avoid a trial where her children would have to testify. They laid her on a sharp rock, put a door on her, and loaded it with rocks and stones, killing her within fifteen minutes. This was March 25, 1586, a Good Friday. *St. Margaret Clitherow*, The Catholic Encyclopedia, http://www.newadvent.org/cathen/04059b.htm (last visited Feb. 28, 2008).

Saint Margaret Clitherow

 In America, the judges employed *peine forte et dure* during the Salem witch trials to kill those who would not plead to being a witch. Giles Corey died from *peine forte et dure* on September 19, 1692, after he refused to enter a plea. According to legend, his last words were *"more weight,"* and he died as the weight was applied. Arthur Miller's political drama The Crucible has Giles Corey refuse to answer "aye or nay" to witchcraft, but the movie version has him killed for refusing to reveal a source of information. The U.S. Constitution prohibits *"corruption of blood"* (i.e., preventing heirs for receiving the condemned's property and rights) in three prohibitions against bills of attainder: *"no Bill of Attainder . . . shall be passed . . . ,"* art. I, § 9, cl. 3; *"No State shall . . . pass any Bill of Attainder . . . ,"* art. I, § 10, cl. 1; and *"[t]he Congress shall have Power to declare the Punishment of Treason, but no Attainder of Treason shall work Corruption of Blood, or Forfeiture except during the Life of the Person attainted,"* art. III, § 3, cl. 2. See Jacob Reynolds, *The Rule of Law and the Origins of the Bill of Attainder Clause,* 18 St. Thomas L. Rev. 177 (2005).

Giles Cory pressed to death during the Salem witch trials

13. Mckenzie at 282. As late as 1772 silence lead to an automatic contempt conviction rather than imposition of compulsory jury trial. Baker at 509.

In 1827 Parliament changed a mute plea to not guilty, the modern practice.[1]

Given the state of pleading in 1649, John Lilburne, an artful government critic, decided to play with his judges.

His judges had to try Lilburne because Cromwell wanted it but needed Lilburne to consent to the court's jurisdiction by pleading *"by God and by country."* Also, his case was too high-profile and political to press a plea out of him.

When asked to plead Lilburne stated:

"By the known laws of England, and a legal jury of my equals, constituted according to the law."

Lilburne was not following the formula.

His judges had to persuade him to say the *"by God and by country"* but Lilburne, being Lilburne, had to add,

". . . that is to say, by a jury of my equals, according to the good old laws of the land." [2]

What the heck, he knew they were there to kill him, so why not have some fun? Besides, Lilburne was playing to the jury.

THE JURY: THE JEWEL IN THE COMMON—LAW CROWN

Before there were police, prosecutors, defense attorneys, and professional judges, the jury was there! Sure, it was not exactly today's institution, but the basics of what a jury does and stands for existed: the conscience of the community.[3]

Although discussed, second-guessed, and often criticized, the trial jury is still with us after centuries.

JURIES IN ATHENS AND ROME

Athenians and Romans had

---

1. *See,* for example, Federal Rule of Criminal Procedure 11(a)(4), which states *"Failure to Enter a Plea. If a defendant refuses to enter a plea . . . the court must enter a plea of not guilty."*

To plead or not to plead, that is the question! Nowhere does the Constitution provide a defendant the right to a plea agreement. Rather, both the original Constitution (at U.S. CONST. art. 3, § 2) and the Bill of Rights (at U.S. CONST. amends. VI, VII) guarantee the defendant a trial. But in any given jurisdiction some 95 to 99 percent of all cases end in a plea bargain. Without plea bargaining the American system of justice would collapse. Prosecutors clear their caseload and can put their resources toward other cases. Those standing for reelection can tout their high conviction rate even though it does not come from

Galileo facing the Roman Inquisition by Cristiano Banti (1857)

trial victories. Despite belief that plea bargaining "lets criminals off," this is not necessarily true. Although each defendant acting rationally will try to get the best deal possible, defendants cannot collectively bargain (and their lawyers are prevented ethically from doing so). Through policy, the prosecutor can dictate the outcome of nearly all cases, saving his resources for the very few that go to trial.

What this means is that our American criminal procedure is not as adversarial as we tout. When the defendant accepts a plea bargain he has a "change of plea" hearing where he declares himself guilty. This is an inquisition.

History provides examples of famous plea agreements:
- Galileo in 1633 got house arrest from the Inquisition in exchange for reciting penitential psalms weekly and recanting Copernican heresies.
- Al Capone bragged about his light sentence for pleading guilty to tax evasion and Prohibition violations. The judge then declared that the bargain did not bind the court, and

Capone got seven and a half years in Alcatraz.

Al Capone

- To avoid execution, James Earl Ray pled guilty in 1969 to assassinating Martin Luther King Jr. and got ninety-nine years.
- In 1973 Spiro Agnew resigned as vice president and pled no contest to failing to report income and received three years' probation and a $10,000 fine (about one-third of the amount in issue).

James Earl Ray

Spiro Agnew

As for film, John Proctor was offered a plea to avoid hanging but has to confront honor and faith in THE CRUCIBLE (20th Century Fox 1996). AND JUSTICE FOR ALL (Columbia Pictures 1979) slams the criminal justice system and the ugliness of plea bargaining, ending with Al Pacino being dragged from the courtroom screaming *"Wanna make a deal!"*

jury trials. For example, in the trial of Socrates, the central theme of Plato's *Euthyphro*, *Apology*, *Crito*, and *Phaedo*, Socrates had a jury of 500 Athenians to decide charges he had corrupted the youth and encouraged them to disbelieve in the ancestral gods. The jury voted to convict 280 to 220. The Athenians also had jury sentencing, with the jury voting 360 to 141 for death.[4]

Athenian juries were drawn at random from citizens. The Athenian playwright Aristophanes described the pharisaical jury practice in his comedy *The Wasps*. Athenian juries valued character evidence, often ignoring the formal law for equitable justice.[5] In most cases these jurors decided the punishment and, like in Socrates's case, they would hear the defendant's second speech regarding punishment.[6]

In ancient Athens you could actually make a modest living as a juror. Jurors got three *obols* per day, approximately one-third of a skilled artisan's daily wage, and the courts were open approximately 150 to 200 days a year.[7]

The Athenians also gave us the earliest known courtroom drama, Aeschylus's *The Oresteia*.[8] Following a really bad family dynamic, Orestes killed his mother for killing his father for killing his sister (Clytemnestra, Agamemnon, and Iphigenia, respectively— that's a family that puts a capital "D" in *dysfunctional!*). The Goddess Athena summoned ten Athenian citizens and bound them by oath to decide Orestes's fate for killing his mom. When they deadlocked, Athena broke the tie by voting not guilty. The Furies, representing punitive vengeance rather than the rule of law, hiss at the verdict, which is common even today with a not guilty verdict.[9]

2. *See* Harold W. Wolfram, *John Lilburne: Democracy's Pillar of Fire*, 3 Syracuse L. Rev. 213, 234–35 and n.79 (1952) (an excellent account of the Lilburne trial and its aftermath).

3. *See, for example, Ring v. Arizona*, 536 U.S. 584 (2002), deciding that juries, not judges, as the true conscience of the community, should decide on the death penalty.

4. The Death of Socrates. The higher number that voted for death shows that he should have had a mitigation lawyer under the American Bar Association standards, requiring two qualified counsel in every death case. For instance, a mitigation lawyer would have told him he should not have argued that instead of death he deserved meals at public expense for being a philosopher. *Apology,* The Works of Plato 60 (Irwin Edman ed., Benjamin Jowett trans., Random House 1956). But Socrates did end up as a character in Bill & Ted's Excellent Adventure (Orion Pictures 1989).

5. Adriaan Lanni, *"Verdict Most Just": The Modes of Classical Athenian Justice,* 16 Yale J.L. & Human. 277, 278 (2004) (*"The Athenians . . . thought giving juries unlimited discretion to reach verdicts based on the particular circumstances of each case was the most just way to resolve disputes."*). Use of character evidence in modern trials is much more limited. *See, e.g.,* Fed. R. Evid. 608.
    See also Jeffrey Omar Usman, *Ancient and Modern Character Evidence: How Character Evidence Was Used in Ancient Athenian Trials, Its Uses in the United States, and What This Means for How These Democratic Societies Understood the Role of Jurors*, 33 Okla. City U. L. Rev. 1 (2008).

6. *Id.* This practice was known as *timesis.*

7. *See* Usman at n.5.

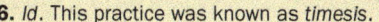
The Remorse of Orestes (1862), as he is pursued by the Furies

Murder of Agamemnon

Nancy Grace

8. Kadri at 4.

The goddess Athena, patroness of Athens

The Sacrifice of Iphigenia

9. Kadri at 5.
    For a modern hissing fury, *see Nancy Grace* (HLN Feb. 21, 2005–present), criticizing any defense verdict.

But despite the dissenting voices, *The Oresteia* reflects two important concepts about law:

1. That the rule of law ends the cycle of revenge murders, which went so far as Orestes's matricide of Clytemnestra.[1]

2. That ordinary men, rather than officials, have the power to judge.[2] Sure, they had an assist from Athena at the end, but those ordinary men coming together to resolve the cycle of violence was something special—a jury!

The ancient Romans had jury trials from the Roman Republic through the early Roman Empire. Juries ranged from 32 to 360 members, with 75 the most common size.[3]

The jurors were drawn from various social classes of free Romans. From the late Roman period into the Middle Ages, Roman courts switched to an early inquisitorial model, with public magistrates instead of juries deciding most issues. The courts would, however, call groups of "*vicini*" ("neighbors") for information on local facts or the reputations of the parties. As we will see, using locals as a form of proof extended from Roman Britain to the Anglo-Saxons and Normans.[4] In fact, some scholars argue that the Romans leaving Britain earlier than the rest of Europe, while Rome was still using this practice of calling *vicini*, is the origin of the later split between the English common-law jury system and the European inquisition.[5]

THE JURY'S SOURCE: FRANKISH, ENGLISH, SCANDINAVIAN, ANGLO—SAXON, OR NORMAN?

Taking the Roman *vicini* and adding various barbarian customs of tribal justice gives a number of possible sources for our jury. Scholars have argued that the jury's origin is Frankish, Scandinavian, Anglo-Saxon, Danish, or Norman.[6] The Swedes, Low Countries, and northern France, especially Normandy, used some type of jury from the twelfth century before Roman-canonical procedure took over.[7]

The jury's origin, from the Normans to England or from the English to Normandy, became an issue later in history.[8] During the seventeenth century, especially

---

1. Susan Ford Wiltshire, Greece, Rome, and the Bill of Rights 156 (1992).

2. Kadri at 6.

3. O.F. Robinson, The Criminal Law of Ancient Rome 4 (1995). *Also* Roscoe Pound, The Lawyer from Antiquity to Modern Times 42 (1951) (noting the size of Roman juries was from 32 to 75). *See also* Wiltshire at 152, stating that Roman courts called "*iudicia publica*" or also "*quaestiones*" were, by Cicero's day, permanent courts presided over by "*praetors*" and having large juries that decided by majority vote.

4. *See* Mike MacNair, *Vicinage and the Antecedents of the Jury*, 17 Law & Hist. Rev. 537, 537–38 (1999). *Compare* Patrick Wormald, *Neighbors, Courts, and Kings: Reflections on Michael Macnair's Vicini*, 17 Law & Hist. Rev. 597 (1999).

5. *See* Bryce Lyon, A Constitutional and Legal History of Medieval England 14 (1960).

6. *See* Ralph V. Turner, *The Origins of the Medieval Jury: Frankish, English, or Scandinavian?* 7 J. Brit. Stud. 1 (1968) (outlining the debate and scholarship).

7. *See* Van Caenegem at 71 (regarding these antecedents), 73 (regarding the Franks and

the Carolingian monarchy as a source). Macnair outlines the scholarship, especially relating to the Norman claim as the jury source. *See also* Turner at 5–7; Charles H. Haskins, *The Early Norman Jury*, 8 Am. Hist. Rev. 613 (1903); James B. Thayer, *The Jury and Its Development*, 5 Harv. L. Rev. 249 (1891–92); Baker at 72; Barnes at 349 and n.26, (arguing that the king's court and the Norman inquest system eventually developed into the jury trial).

8. *See* MacNair at 539–40. *See generally* John Phillip Reid, The Ancient Constitution and the Origins of Anglo-American Liberty (2005).

9. But see Pollack at 189, attacking the myth of the "ancient" Anglo-Saxon constitution and arguing that most of the jury system came out of the Norman inquest procedures, not from King Alfred.

10. *Quoted in* Wolfram at 246.

11. Thomas Jefferson, for instance, adopted the theory that the English common law was the ancient pre-Norman law of Saxon England. Howe at 584.

12. The Sixth Amendment states:

"*In all criminal prosecutions, the accused shall enjoy the right to a speedy and public trial, by an impartial jury...*"

And the Seventh Amendment amplifies:

Norman 15th Century Jury of 12 with court officials

during the struggles with the Stuart monarchs and their notions of absolute monarchy, democratic proponents like the Puritans asserted "*Anglo-Saxon liberty*" and the "*ancient constitution*" as the legacy of all Englishmen against the "Norman" kingship.[9]

John Lilburne, for example, in his 1649 trial played to these themes with the jury, asserting his "*Anglo-Saxon liberty*."

When Lilburne argued the jury decided the law, one of his judges, Lord Keble, responded with indignation that the jury

"*judges matter(s) of fact . . . not . . . law.*"

Lilburne responded that

"*the jury by law are not only judges of fact, but of law also; and you call yourselves judges of the law, are no more but Norman intruders; and in deed and in truth, if the jury please, are no more but ciphers, to pronounce their verdict.*" (Emphasis added.)

Keble did not like being called a cipher, decrying,

"*was there ever such a damnable blasphemous heresy as this is, to call the judges of the law, ciphers?*"[10]

But, as we will see, Lilburne knew that his audience was the jury.

The American Founding Fathers adopted Lilburne's ideal[11] and enshrined it in both the Sixth and Seventh Amendments.[12]

WHY TWELVE?

The Anglo-American trial settled on twelve jurors to unanimously decide the fate of criminal defendants. Sir Edward Coke explained that the "*number of twelve is much respected in holy writ, as 12 apostles, 12 stones, 12 tribes, etc.*"[13] Coke recognized that in our Judeo-Christian culture, twelve is an important number.[14]

The connection with the twelve apostles or the twelve tribes of Israel seems an obvious precedent.[15] Reflecting this biblical origin, trial by compurgation generally required the defendant's oath with eleven compurgators, totaling twelve oaths, which could have been the origin of the modern twelve-juror rule.[16] We do know, for instance, that in 879 AD King Alfred the Great signed a peace treaty with King Guthrum of Denmark establishing that a killer in both realms could cleanse himself of the blood guilt by producing twelve sworn men.[17]

"In Suits at common law, where the value in controversy shall exceed twenty dollars, the right of trial by jury shall be preserved, and no fact tried by a jury, shall be otherwise re-examined in any Court of the United States, than according to the rules of the common law."

13. *Quoted in* WILTSHIRE at 162.

The Bill of Rights in the U.S. National Archives

14. "Twelve" is a native English word from the Germanic compound "*twa-lif*" ("two-leave," i.e., two is left after taking ten). Moreover, twelve is the last number before the formulaic thirteen, fourteen, etc. Twelve has its own name, a "dozen," reflected in the movies CHEAPER BY THE DOZEN (20th Century Fox 1950, and again in 2003) and THE DIRTY DOZEN (MGM 1967). There are twelve months in a year, twelve inches in a foot, twelve hours on a clock, and twelve days of Christmas. Twelve times twelve is a "gross," and twelve is between lucky eleven and unlucky thirteen. There are twelve signs in the zodiac (the Chinese zodiac as well) and twelve Olympian gods in Greek mythology. Although hardly a highbrow legal argument, all these twelves show that it is just not a good idea to have less than twelve jurors.

The twelve Olympian gods

The zodiac

15. The Twelve Apostles (thirteenth century). As G.K. Chesterton wrote, "*Our civilization has decided, and very justly decided that determining the guilt or innocence of men is a thing too important to be trusted to trained men. If it wishes for light upon that awful matter, it asks men who know no more law than I know, but who can feel the things I felt in the jury box. When it wants a library catalogued, or the solar system discovered, or a trifle of that kind, it uses up its specialists. But when it wishes anything done that is really serious, it collects twelve of the ordinary men standing about. The same thing was done, if I remember right, by the Founder of Christianity.*" G.K. CHESTERTON, TREMENDOUS TRIFLES 86 (1968), *quoted in* Phillip B. Scott, *Jury Nullification: An Historical Perspective on a Modern Debate*, 91 W. VA. L. REV. 389 (1988).

16. MacNair at 573; MacNair at 15. For the Supreme Court's acknowledgement of compurgation roots, see *Apodaca v. Oregon*, 406 U.S. 404, 408 nn. 2 & 3 (1972), discussed in Ethan J. Leib, *Supermajoritarianism and the American Criminal Jury*, 33 HASTINGS CONST. L.Q. 141–42 (2006).

12 ANGRY MEN (United Artists 1957), the classic jury drama

17. KADRI at 71.

Also, the Anglo-Saxons and Danes had their twelve "*thegns*" ("*thanes*") sitting as a sort of early grand jury deciding whether a defendant would face trial by ordeal or battle.

But leaving aside historical arguments, it could just be that the English didn't like the decimal system, as shown by the fact that there used to be twelve pence to a shilling.[1]

THE EARLY ENGLISH JURY

The first recorded jury trial was in 1220 at Westminster. From there, the circuit judges took the procedure with them to the "*shires*" ("counties").[2] By the middle of the thirteenth century the trial by jury, at least in an early form, was standard.[3]

The Westminster trial of 1220, however, was probably not the first jury trial. The early jury system replaced the older form of accusation called an appeal, from the Latin verb "to name."[4] In England, private prosecutions were called "*appeals*," originally meaning an accusation. As the jury system emerged, the word "*appeal*" came to mean trial by jury without option of battle.[5]

The early jury was both our modern grand jury and trial jury. In modern practice the *grand* jury decides

---

1. WILTSHIRE at 161.

A shilling was an English unit of currency; it is still used in some former British Commonwealth countries. "Shilling" comes from "*schilling*," a term from Anglo-Saxon times relating to the value of a cow or sheep. Originally, twenty shillings made a British pound, and twelve pence made a shilling. Thus there were 240 pence in a pound.

The new five pence piece initially was of identical size and weight, had the same value, and inherited the shilling's slang name of a "bob."

A 1933 shilling

2. KADRI at 70.

3. Frederick Pollack, *The King's Peace in the Middle Ages*, 13 HARV. L. REV. 177, 187 (1899).

Magna Carta did not provide for criminal jury trials for everyone, only that barons would be tried by their peers. At the time only if a person was indicted by a grand jury could he have another jury. LOVELL at 116. Only later did *Magna Carta* become a symbol that the law is superior to men, including the king and his government. *Id.* at 118.

4. LOVELL at 109.

5. Klerman, *Settlement*, at 3; Pollack at 179.

6. The word "indictment" probably comes from the Latin "*indicare*," meaning "to point a finger," as in the more common modern English word "indicate." By the fourteenth century, it had come to mean a written accusation after formal inquiry. See BAKER at 505.

Of course, your "index" finger has the same origin.

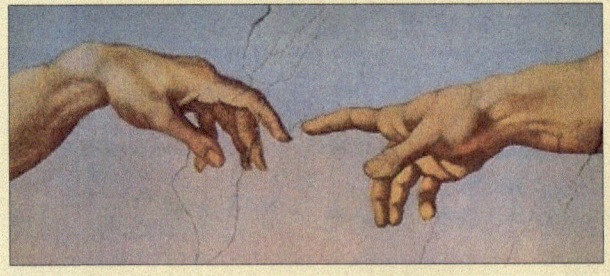

Michelangelo's God uses his index finger to give Adam life

7. See SHAPIRO at 2. *Also* Kiralfy at 246; Groot, *Presentment*, at 1; BAKER at 73.

Raphael's Plato indicating up

Da Vinci's John the Baptist indicating God

whether a charge stands, called an "indictment,"[6] and the trial or *petit* jury decides guilt or innocence.

At least before Henry II, the early jury could exonerate an accused, condemn him, or send him to trial by ordeal.[7] Generally the early jury sent the accused to ordeal if it was unsure of guilt.[8] Thus it acted initially like a modern grand jury. The jury's opinion about guilt or innocence was still a verdict.

These jurors were essentially witnesses called to the "*eyre*," the periodic session of the royal county court.[9] They came from the "*hundred*" and "*vill*," each a smaller subdivision of the *shire*.[10] This truly was a jury "*of your peers*."[11] And these jurors testified; they came to court expecting to speak more than to listen.

Thus, from Norman times and perhaps even earlier, the jurors were self-

informed; they knew the parties and the facts. The judges knew less about the case than the jurors.[12] In fact several members of a trial jury may have been part of making the indictment or complaint, or were coroners, bailiffs, and constables.[13] "Witnesses," as we know them, only occasionally came to court.[14] The jury was therefore mainly a form of proof, not the decider of proof.[15]

8. Kerr at 577–78; *see also* VAN CAENEGEM at 62. Naomi D. Hurnard, *The Jury of Presentment and the Assize of Clarendon*, 56 ENG. HIST. REV. 374 (1941).

9. *See* Daniel Klerman, *Was the Jury Ever Self-Informing?* 77 S. CAL. L. REV. 123, n.29 (2003); Groot, *Prosecutions*, at 125–40 (describing the eyre). *See also* Justin C. Barnes, *Lessons Learned from England's "Great Guardian of Liberty": A Comparative Study of English and American Civil Juries*, 3 U. ST. THOMAS L.J. 345, 350 (2005); Margaret C. Klingelsmith, *New Readings of Old Law*, 66 U. PA. L. REV. 107 (1917–18).

10. Groot, *Presentment*, at 3 and n.9. The *hundred* was an Anglo-Saxon organization of "*hundredors*" (more or less ten "*tithing*" families) that paid the frankpledge (tax). The "*hundredarius*" (family head) would meet in the "*hundred gemote*" headed by the "*hundredary*." BLACK's at 667. The *vill* was a smaller unit than the *hundred*, such as a parish, manor, or tithing. *See id.* at 1407. Both the words "village" and "villain" (referring to an unfree inhabitant of a *vill*) come from *vill*.

11. For more on jury composition, *see* Klerman, *Self-Informing Jury*, at 128. The Sixth Amendment reflects this in its requirement that the juries come from "*the State and district wherein the crime shall have been committed . . .*" This phrase is anachronistic, relating to *hundreds* and *vills*.

12. Klerman, *Self-Informing Jury*, at 127, 138; Shapiro at 4; Barnes at 350; Klingelsmith at 107; Kerr at 576–77. Through early modern times, the special jury remained a throwback to self-informed juries. *See* James C. Oldham, *The Origins of the Special Jury*, 50 U. CHI. L. REV. 137 (1983).

14. Klerman, *Self-Informing Jury*, at 136, 145 (demonstrating the relationship with compurgation).

15. MacNair at 548–49. The jury as a form of proof can still be seen in modern practice, where the jury renders the verdict but not the judgment, a function of the trial judge.
   Klerman gives several examples of this from a thirteenth century treatise, THE PLACITA CORONE (c. 1274–75). Reproducing one example here shows both the nature of trials and the role of jurors and judges:
   Judge: *Thomas [the accused], you have greatly embroidered your tale and coloured your defense: for you are telling us only what you think will be to your advantage, and suppressing whatever you think may damage you, and I do not believe you have told the whole truth.*
   Thomas: *Sir, I have told the whole truth, and related the affair from the beginning to the end in every detail: and of this I trust myself to God and the country for both good and evil.*

13. Jurors were not passive note takers, like today, but more like witnesses. *See* Musson at 127–28, 142 (outlining the difficulty of getting jurors in the fourteenth century).

   To resolve this dispute, the judge called an "inquest" with a jury, which agreed with Thomas:
   Judge: *Thomas, these good people testify by their oaths to the truth of what you have said. So our judgment is that what you did to him, you did in self defense.*
   Quoted in Klerman, *Settlement*, at 136. In Thomas's trial the judge rendered "*our judgment*" but only after the jury gave proof by "*their oaths.*" It essentially appears as a form of compurgation. *See also* Morris S. Arnold, *Law and Fact in Medieval Jury Trials: Out of Sight, Out of Mind*, 18 AM. J. LEGAL HIST. 267, 279–80 (1974) (noting that law and fact for medieval jurors were essentially the same thing—*ex facto ius, ex jure factum*).

The jurors took an oath to give a true verdict.[1] Indeed, the very word "jury" comes from the Latin "*jurata*" ("an oath"), with "jurors" being "*juratores.*" [2] This oath had great weight and negated the fact that jurors customarily received "gifts" from both parties, probably more akin to what we would think of as a jury fee, for their service.[3]

The jurors also investigated the case, returning to testify as to what they had discovered and to make accusations.[4] In fact the oath of the early jurors, the antecedents of the oaths of today's petit and grand jurors, came from their oath to investigate crime and "present" it to the king for prosecution.[5] In this function the early jury was a precursor to police and prosecutors.[6]

Henry II and his successors saw one great advantage in the jury system—it was cheap.

The self-informed jury of unpaid laymen did all the hard and expensive work of what we today would call criminal investigation, civil discovery, and trial preparation.[7] The kings then collected the death taxes and court fees in civil cases and the hefty fines and forfeitures in criminal cases.

Justice was a moneymaker!

But the kings did have to provide for the procedure. At first they traveled around the realm directly dispensing justice. Later they sent judges to periodically exercise the king's authority in the counties, diminishing the authority of the local lord and church. All of this was the extension of the king's peace.[8]

This system of witness-jurors lasted into the fifteenth century.[9] The early English courts, in fact, frowned on our modern idea of a witness as an independent observer of events. In the 1470s Sir

---

1. Kerr at 575–76.

The word "verdict" comes from the Latin "*veredictum*" ("to tell the truth," that is, "*vere*," as in the English word "verify," and "*dictum*," as in the English word "dictate"), reflecting the duty of the jurors. Baker at 72.

A jury oath from 1642 read as follows: "*You shall well and truly try, and true deliverance make between our Soveraign [sic] Lord the King, and the Prisoners at the Bar, whom you shall have in charge, and a true Verdict shall give according to your Evidence, so help you God.*"

Quoted in James Oldham, *Truth-Telling in the Eighteenth-Century English Courtroom*, 12 Law & Hist. Rev. 95, 106 n.58 (1994). Modern jury oaths are similar and even retain the "*so help you God,*" essentially *iusticium Dei*. Indeed, before the Elizabethan Perjury Statute of 1563, the only perjury punishable at common law was against jurors for giving dishonest verdicts (testimony). Michael D. Gordon, *The Perjury Statute of 1563: A Case History of Confusion*, 124 Proc. Am. Phil. Soc'y 438 (1980).

The Verdict (20th Century Fox 1982) is about a washed-up, alcoholic lawyer, played by Paul Newman, who gets one last case to save his career. The dramatic buildup is to the jury verdict.

The Verdict (Warner Brothers 1946) is a film noir, starring Sydney Greenstreet as a Scotland Yard detective investigating a murder with Peter Lorre as his friend.

The best movie showing a jury actually deliberating is 12 Angry Men, though Philadelphia (TriStar Pictures 1993) has a brief but informative jury deliberation scene.

2. Baker at 72–73; Pollock at 188. For the comparison of the juror's oaths with the oaths taken by witnesses and compurgators, *see* Baker at 75. *See also* Stephan Landsman, *The Civil Jury in America: Scenes from an Unappreciated History*, 44 Hastings L.J. 579, 584–85 (1993).

3. Musson at 132 and n.150. It was not until 1682 that it became punishable to contact or inform jurors outside court proceedings of any fact or law regarding a case before them. Landsman at 586.

4. Until Henry II became king in 1154, the jury was mostly an administrative institution in the king's governance. It was only after Henry II passed several statutes, called assizes, that the jury started to become an instrument of justice. Landsman at 583.

5. Pollack at 187.

6. Pollack at 181; Howard W. Goldstein, Grand Jury Practice 2-1 to 2-2 (2005); Groot, *Presentment*, at 4–5; Barnes at 350, 356. On Norman practices, *see* Thompson at 21.

John Fortescue wrote in *De Laudibus Legum Angliae* that witnesses were sinister because they could lie or be bribed to say anything, whereas twelve sworn *"good men and true"* could not. Because England relied on jurors and did not torture witnesses, he continued, its legal system was better than the Continental inquisition.[10] It was the jurors' specific oath to give a true verdict, rather than the judge, that served as the accused's main procedural protection.

These juror-witnesses implemented the social norms of their day. For instance, they would have known to whom a disputed cow belonged or, perhaps, to whom it *should* belong. For example, even if the cow technically belonged to Thomas, Hugh may have had a better right or need to it. Or maybe Hugh was just a nicer guy than Thomas. Juries could take this into account.

In a criminal case the juror-witness would have known before trial who killed whom. But the jury's verdict, the oath-bound duty to tell and implement the truth, accounted for all the complicated nuances of modern law, such as self-defense, accident, manslaughter, or first- and second-degree murder. If you were a defendant before a medieval jury you had a better chance than you have today of getting mercy. The jurors knew the punishments and thus effectively were the sentencers.[11]

Fortescue described

"who, then, in England can be put to death unjustly for any crime? Since he is allowed so many pleas and privileges in favor of life; none but his neighbors, men of honest and good repute, against whom he can have no probable cause of exception, can find the person accused guilty." [12]

In 12 ANGRY MEN Henry Fonda brings his own exhibit into the jury room, not admitted into evidence during the trial. The Norman jury system would have required this action. Today it is juror misconduct.

7. Landsman at 584; LOVELL at 86.

8. See *The Sixth Amendment* from this series, Constitution Press, 2017.

9. KADRI at 72; Klerman, *Settlement*, at 6 (noting that juries remained self-informed throughout the thirteenth and fourteenth centuries).

10. KADRI at 73.
The engraved frontispiece from *De Laudibus Legum Angliae* shows Fortescue with Prince Edward in France, and reads: "Chancellor Fortescue following King Henry's Fortune, and attending his Son Edward into France, wrote this Book to recommend the Laws of England to the Esteem and Protection of that Young Prince." From the Boston College Law School website, http://images.google.com/imgres?imgurl=http://www.bc.edu/schools/law/library/meta-elements/jpg/FortescueTPfullsize.jpg&imgrefurl=http://www.bc.edu/schools/law/library/about/rarebook/exhibitions/newacq05.html&usg=__Dyk UvoTXBJDHlvQOAU59Pbcid28=&h=3504&w=2548&sz=1 354&hl=en&start=15&tbnid=7EUBSgRbBH3sKM:&tbnh =150&tbnw=109&prev=/images%3Fq%3DJohn%2BForte scue%26gbv%3D2%26ndsp%3D21%26hl%3Den%26sa% 3DN (last visited Dec. 5, 2009).

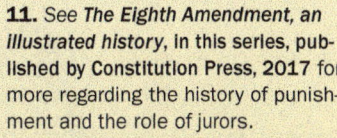

11. See *The Eighth Amendment, an Illustrated history*, in this series, published by Constitution Press, 2017 for more regarding the history of punishment and the role of jurors.

12. *Coffin v. United States*, 156 U.S. 432, 455 (1895), quoting Fortescue and citing *De Laudibus Legum Angliae* (Amos trans., Cambridge Univ. Press, 1825). What follows this quote is Fortescue's statement that "one would much rather that twenty guilty persons should escape the punishment of death than that one innocent person should be condemned and suffer capitally."

Sir John Fortescue

It was rough justice, but justice nonetheless.

THE GRAND JURY AND PETIT JURY

In 1166, Henry II's Assize of Clarendon provided that after the jury of presentment, the case went to ordeal.[1] If Henry II wished by this reform to impose justice, this motive was secondary to asserting his power over church and barons, and making income from forfeited chattels of convicted felons.[2]

The Assize of Clarendon set up a purely accusatorial jury of twelve men to ferret out crime and "keep the peace."[3]

When this jury initiated a case it was a "*presentment*" to the king, as distinguished from an "*indictment*," which came when the prosecutor gave the case to the jury.[4]

The language of this early grand jury showed its investigative role— it would issue a "*bulla vera*" ("a true bill") if it had a charge or a "*bulla ignoramus*" ("it was ignorant," meaning there was not enough evidence) if they had no charge.[5] The charges were organized in "*counts*," from the French "*conte*" ("tale" or "story").[6]

If there was any doubt as to Henry II's purpose, he

heavily fined grand juries or their villages that failed to indict a suspect or to present a sufficient number of criminals.[7]

In 1215 a crisis in criminal procedure occurred. As noted, the church held the Fourth Lateran Council, prohibiting clergy participation in the ordeal, effectively ending it as a mode of trial. At this point the English presentment juries had to send the case somewhere. The answer was a smaller jury, namely, the "*petit*" (French for "small") jury, which we today call the "trial jury."[8] *Magna Carta* may have

1. Here the term "assize" has a meaning closer to the modern words "ordinance" or "decree" than a court session, though at this time they were all court sessions from the king's court. Henry II issued this decree after the Constitution of Clarendon and Northampton, which Archbishop Thomas Becket had repudiated because it infringed on church jurisdiction. Goldstein at 2-4. In this case the decree attempted to prevent the abusive practice of bringing laymen before the bishop after an anonymous accusation. *See* Schwartz at 707.

Henry II

2. Schwartz at 703–10 (noting various power struggles between Henry II and Becket, and Henry's attempts to wrest power from the English barons). *See also* Goldstein at 2-3 and 2-5; United States v. Navarro, 408 F.3d 1184, 1190 (9th Cir. 2005).

3. Baker at 24; Bellamy at 19. For the Assize of Clarendon and Constitution of Clarendon, see http://www.constitution.org/ liberlib.htm (last visited June 1, 2007).

4. *Navarro*, 408 F.3d at 1190; Bellamy at 23. The early grand jury, representatives from the *hundreds* and *vills*, presented the case to the traveling royal judges. Baker at 24. This "presentment" to the king is why we still refer to an indictment as being "handed up." *See also* Thompson at 15. The first clause of the Fifth Amendment requires either an indictment or a presentiment: "*No person shall be held to answer for a capital, or otherwise infamous crime, unless on a presentment or indictment of a Grand Jury . . .*"

5. Schwartz at 718; Bellamy at 20, 46; Baker at 505. *See also* David Crook, *Triers and the Origin of the Grand Jury*, 12 J. Legal Hist. 103 (1991) (tracing the evolution from available records of jurors from indictors to "*triatores*" or "trial juries").

6. As in the root of the English verb "to recount." Baker at 76. The Latin is "*narratio*," as in the English word "narrative."

7. Schwartz at 709. Only much later did it become illegal to fine jurors. *See* Goldstein at 2-6.
   Henry II's expansion of existing jury custom is why he gets credited with being the founder of the jury trial. Kiralfy at 241. *See also* Bellamy at 33, noting that the Statute of Westminster of 1285 allowed the king to punish jurors or their villages for negligence or concealing felonies. Jury service could not have been popular given that in the fourteenth and fifteenth centuries an acquitted defendant could sue jurors who indicted him. *Id.* at 34.

8. *See* Baker at 507–08; Shapiro at 4; Schwartz at 711 and n.47; Kiralfy at 248. On grand juries and petit juries forming a two-staged system, see Helmholz, *Grand Jury*, at 613. *See also* Baker at 73 on the effect of the Fourth Lateran Council on the development of the petit jury.

been the foundation for this right to trial by jury.[9] *Vox populi* ("the people's voice") replaced *vox Dei* ("God's voice") as a mode of trial.[10]

This split developed a two-tiered system that Blackstone later noted

> "*wisely placed this strong and twofold barrier, of a presentment and a trial by jury between the liberties of the people and the prerogative of the crown.*"[11]

Blackstone's influence on law and lawyers in the colonies, firmly planted this concept of a jury trial in the minds of the Constitution's Framers.

THE CHANGING ROLE OF THE GRAND JURY

The trouble with Blackstone's view of the grand jury as "*a barrier*" for the "*liberties of the people*" is that the jury's early history belies it.

Henry II formalized the grand jury system because he wanted to gain power and money. Common people did not see the grand jury as a barrier to the king; rather, they feared it.[12] Not until the middle of the fourteenth

century were grand jurors excluded from serving on trial juries for the same cases where they had just indicted a defendant.[13]

Henry II's successors carried on the grand jury practice. By the fourteenth century under Edward III, the grand jury became institutionalized with the number of grand jurors set at twenty-four and got the title "*le graunde inquest.*"[14]

Over time, the grand jury became an instrument of governance rather than a barrier to it.[15]

---

9. "*No freeman shall be taken or imprisoned or disseised or exiled or in any way destroyed, nor will we go upon him nor send upon him, except by the lawful judgment of his peers or by the law of the land.*" *Magna Carta* of 1215.

(This clause could refer to either the grand or the petit jury.) *Cited in* Barnes at 348. *See also* GOLDSTEIN at 2-5 to 2-6. Fisher at 585 (noting record of first jury trial in 1220). For a general explanation of the *Magna Carta* in medieval law, *see* Paul R. Hyams, *The Charter as a Source for the Early Common Law*, 12 J. LEGAL HIST. 173 (1991).

Isabella and a young Edward III

10. VAN CAENEGEM at 71. From 1351 the trial jurors had to be different from the grand jurors. BAKER at 508. We extend this rule today to assure that evidence presented to a grand jury, not necessarily admissible at trial or perhaps illegally obtained, will not taint the trial.

11. Schwartz at 701.

12. Schwartz at 709 ("*Any thought that the grand juries were for the benefit of the people must be quickly dispelled by the historic fact that the grand jury was oppressive and much feared by the common people.*"). *See also* GOLDSTEIN at 2-1 to 2-2, noting that the grand jury has at different times been both the government's sword and the citizen's shield.

14. Roger A. Fairfax, Jr., *The Jurisdictional Heritage of the Grand Jury Clause*, 91 MINN. L. REV. 398, 408 n.39 (2006) (quoting GEORGE J. EDWARDS, THE GRAND JURY: AN ESSAY 2 (1906)); Pollack at 188 (noting that the grand jury came from "the grand inquest"). From the reign of Edward III also came inquisitorial trial procedures, which could have ended the jury trial tradition. BELLAMY at 14–15. Edward III was a successful king who beat up on the French and Scots. His mother was Isabella (known as the She-Wolf of France), who was the princess in BRAVEHEART. *See* ALISON WEIR, QUEEN ISABELLA (2005). Edward's son, Edward, known as the Black Prince, died before becoming king but he was the prince in A KNIGHT'S TALE (Columbia Pictures 2001), played by James Purefoy.

William Blackstone

13. Pollack at 181.

Edward III and his son Edward, the Black Prince

15. From the seventeenth century the grand jury began to acquire powers beyond justice administration. It maintained roads and bridges, collected county cess and taxes, oversaw lunatic asylums, hospitals, and jails, and became an elected body. GOLDSTEIN at 2-8; Navarro, 408 F.3d at 1191. This was especially true in colonial America.

The grand jury of Blackstone's time that the Framers knew truly did stand against the power of the government. Today, though, the grand jury is totally under the prosecutor's control, who has sweeping powers of subpoena and investigation. The grand jury is not the shield for the people's liberties that it once was.[1]

JURIES AND THE KING'S COPS

Juries were now either grand or petit and, as the system formalized, they started to lose their character as bodies with independent knowledge of the facts. More and more the juries did not know directly about cases. Trials were starting to incorporate actual witnesses to give testimony, usually from what we would today call a "cop," a policeman.

Kings actually did not have cops in the modern sense of police officer; the concept of police and policing was centuries away.[2] There was a "constable," but during the Middle Ages this was a high military office.[3] Only later did the term become associated with policing.[4] What the king did have were sheriffs, coroners, and judges.

The Sheriff: The "*sheriff*" was the King's "*reeve*"

---

1. What's So Grand about the Grand Jury? The grand jury is a shell of what it was. The proponents of the American Revolution viewed the grand jury as a shield from government oppression, or in Blackstone's terms, the king's prerogative power. GOLDSTEIN at 2-6. Colonial grand juries refused to indict when the king infringed on the people's liberty. LEVY at 222. *See generally* Fairfax (demonstrating that the Framers intended a grand jury's indictment to be a prerequisite for federal court jurisdiction over a crime and thus should not be something a defendant can waive, as is common in modern plea practice and allowed by Federal Rule of Criminal Procedure 7). Today in America a prosecutor could indict "*a ham sandwich.*" GOLDSTEIN at 2-14; Schwartz at 756–58 (on modern history and prosecutorial tactics). *See generally* Niki Kuckes, *The Democratic Prosecutor: Explaining the Constitutional Function of the Federal Grand Jury*, 94 GEO. L.J. 1265 (2006). England abolished the grand jury, KEMPIN at 54, as have many states of the United States, despite periodic calls for reform. *See, e.g.*, John F. Decker, *Legislating New Federalism: The Call for Grand Jury Reform in the States*, 58 OKLA. L. REV. 341 (2005); Kevin K. Washburn, *Restoring The Grand Jury*, 76 FORDHAM L. REV. 2333 (2008).

2. Sir Robert Peel, Britain's Conservative prime minister, helped create the modern police force in the 1860s while he served as home secretary. The father of modern policing, Peel developed the Peelian Principles, which defined police ethics. His most memorable principle was, "*the police are the public, and the public are the police.*" English police are still called "bobbies" or "'peelers." For the history of the early police and the Bow Street Runners, *see* LOVELL at 509.

3. The constable originally was a stable boy keeping the lord's horses. The word comes from the Latin "*comes stabuli*" ("attendant of the stables"). Later it became a high military rank, the lord high constable of England, essentially the king's field marshal.

Constables also defended castles, and there is still a constable of the Tower of London. *Magna Carta* uses the term in this sense to denote a castellan with less power than the sheriff. *See* Irwin Langbien, *The Jury of Presentment and the Coroner*, 33 COLUM. L. REV. 1329, 1343 n.47 (1933).

4. The term "cop" could be short for "Constable On Patrol." Or it might come from Latin and Old French "*capere*" ("to capture"), hence a "copper," who "cops criminals," or to "cop a plea." "Cop" could also derive from the copper buttons on police uniforms.

"Cop" is now synonymous with "police officer," as in the television show *Cops* that follows police officers, constables, and sheriff's deputies as they police. *Cops* (Fox TV, Mar. 11, 1989–Mar. 21, 2009), http://www.cops.com/ (last visited Apr. 9, 2010). There is also the movie COP (1988) with James Woods.

The use of the phrase "cop a plea" or "cop out to a plea" could come from the fact that the hearing is officially called a "change of plea [to guilty] hearing," and shortened to "COP." The term "cop out" is also synonymous with doing something to avoid responsibility, as in "that's a cop out." The comedy COP OUT (Warner Brothers 2010), however, seems to use the term as a play on the buddy cop theme, as in the two buddies are going *out* on a date.

5. "The Reeve's Tale" is the third of Geoffrey Chaucer's THE CANTERBURY TALES. The reeve of the story, Oswald, is skinny and bad-tempered, and after the previous *Miller's Tale* annoys him, his story has a miller trying to swindle two "students." But they trick the miller's wife and daughter ("representative," "caretaker," or "overseer")[5] in the *shire*, thus his Anglo-Saxon name was "*shire-gerefa*," or in Norman French "*shire-reeve*" (evolving into *sheriff*).[6] It was an older Anglo-Saxon office that the Normans kept. The *sheriff* was supposed to collect the royal revenue.[7]

The only appeal from the *sheriff*, or his courts, was to the king.[8] However, the king was often overseas (and, in the early Norman period,

did not even speak English). Thus the "*justiciar*," "*regent*," or "*lieutenant*" heard the appeal.

As the king's interest in criminal cases grew, the *sheriff* started having a law enforcement role. He would direct the "*hue and cry*" to pursue criminals.[9] He would summon prosecuting victims to court and deliver defendants from jail. Over time he ran the jails, a role country sheriffs still play.

The Coroner: Offsetting some of the *sheriff*'s power was another crown official, the "*coroner*."[10] "*Coroner*" means "keeper of the pleas of the crown" or "crowner" or "coronator."[11] It was his duty to enforce the king's right to forfeited chattel.[12] He did this using an "*inquest*" (in Latin, "*inquisitio*") or coroner's court, often presiding over an early form of jury trial.[13]

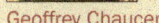

Geoffrey Chaucer

into sex (perhaps willingly) and end up with a nice cake besides. (Who said medieval literature was boring?)

"Students" drinking up a miller's wine in "The Reeve's Tale"

A seventeenth century depiction of Chaucer

6. Van Caenegem at 13; Kynell at 86; Lovell at 33–35; W.A. Morris, *The Sheriff and the Justices of William Rufus and Henry I*, 7 Cal. L. Rev. 235, 240 (1910). *See also* Danziger & Gillingham at 175–76. Regarding the sheriff as the king's representative in the Anglo-Saxon *hundred* and *shire* courts, *see* Pollock at 293. For royal control of the sheriff, *see* Baker at 23.

7. This is the Sheriff of Nottingham of the Robin Hood stories, who takes from the poor to give to the rich.

8. *See* Kynell at 47 (noting how the early jury functioned in the context of the *sheriff*'s inquests).

9. "**Follow that Car!**" The *hue and cry* to pursue criminals led centuries later to the sheriff swearing in a posse and declaring "*They went that 'a way!*" and later ordering a driver to "*Follow that car!*" Lovell at 41.

10. *See* Charles Gross, *The Early History and Influence of the Office of Coroner*, 7 Pol. Sci. Q. 656, 660, 665 (1892); Lovell at 101 (coroner established to check the *sheriffs*). The *coroners* were probably more popular than the *sheriffs* as they were popularly chosen and not just the king's representative. Conversely, *sheriffs* often bought their office intending private gain. Gross at 664.

11. Langbien at 1334. This role as "keeper of the pleas of the crown" used to be the *justiciar*'s. *Id.* at 1341.
      The term "*coroner*" comes from the Latin "*corona*" ("crown"), as in the English "coronation" for the crowning of a monarch. *See also* Corona brand beer for the crown on its label.

12. "**Chattel**" means private movable property or goods, as opposed to "real property," i.e., real estate. The term included "*royal fish*," such as whales, sturgeon, and porpoises caught near or on the shore. *See* Thompson at 32. The word "cattle" derives from "chattel," as it originally referred to any domesticated quadruped livestock, including sheep, goats, swine, horses, mules, and asses, not just today's meaning of bovines, such as steers, cows, and bulls. Webster's at 425–26, 455.
      On the coroner's role in forfeitures to the crown, *see* Gross at 659, and in defending the king's interest against the local lords, *see* Gross at 667.

13. Gross at 663, 672. The inquest jury functioned more as the king's investigatory panel rather than a modern jury. Barnes at 349.

Where a death was involved he would make sure the king got his death tax. If it was a homicide or suicide the king fared even better because *all* the goods and chattels of the murderer or suicide went to him.[1]

This is where the modern understanding of the role of the coroner derives,[2] although most jurisdictions today use trained medical professionals in medical examiners' offices.

For most of the medieval period, the *sheriff* and *coroner* were the extent of law enforcement. But policing was a community matter, and the village had a greater role in ferreting out crime and seeking its prosecution.

The Judges: The king had another cop: the judge.[3] Judges from the Middle Ages had both executive and judicial powers. They were the king's men, and thus responsible for keeping the king's peace.

Not only would the judge examine the witnesses and comment on the evidence, he would often tell the jury what he thought its verdict should be. He could reject the verdict and send the jury to redeliberate or even put the jurors in jail or fine them.[4]

JURORS BECOME EVEN LESS INFORMED

Over time, as juries started coming from larger geographic areas and were comprised of people with less personal knowledge of the parties and the dispute, the jury lost its investigatory role. Jurors did not know the parties, and the parties did not know them.

As William Shakespeare wrote,

> *"the jury passing on the prisoner's life / May in the sworn twelve have a thief or two / Guiltier than him they try."* [5]

Starting with crown officials like *sheriffs* and *coroners*, by the middle of the fifteenth century, jurors had become dependent on in-court testimony.[6] In 1523 Sir Thomas More argued that jurors should only have evidence from the trial.[7]

---

1. Thompson at 31–32. The *coroner's* office probably started under Henry II and is mentioned in *Magna Carta* and the *eyre* of 1194.
See Gross at 656; Langbien at 1334; Barnes at 348–49 (for the tie-in with inquest). In addition, see John H. Wigmore, *The History of the Hearsay Rule*, 17 HARV. L. REV. 437, 456 (1903–04), noting the coroner's inquest as an exception allowing hearsay before justices of the peace.

2. Some states maintain a variant of the old *coroner's* inquest. ▼

3. By the fourteenth century, traveling justices and justices of the peace limited both the sheriff and *coroner's* powers. LOVELL at 206–07.

4. John H. Langbein, *The Criminal Trial before the Lawyers*, 45 U. CHI. L. REV. 263, 291–95 (1977–78).

5. WILLIAM SHAKESPEARE, MEASURE FOR MEASURE act 2, sc. 1, ll. 19–21, *quoted in* KORNSTEIN at 52.

6. Klerman, *Settlement*, at 145–48; Westen at 80–81; Morano at 507.

7. Shapiro at 5. *Also see* Landsman at 587, noting that in the mid-1600s, jurors were isolated from outside influences and required to decide cases on in-court presentations.

Sir Thomas More

Many factors contributed to jurors becoming less self-informed. The courts were becoming more efficient after centralization at Westminster, with formal sessions and terms. The local townsfolk of the *vill* or *hundred* no longer showed up for jury duty whenever an *eyre* justice passed though.[8] The king started enforcing the criminal law with crown officials, ending the need for *le graunde inquest* to investigate and report crime.[9] The Black Death affected judicial institutions, as it did many other social organizations, by limiting the number of jurors but not the obligations of local communities.[10]

By this point another factor limited the self-informed jury. Legal decision making became a rational process.[11] Oaths as a form of proof became harder to justify, and *iudicium Dei* was on the wane. The king's judges now instructed the jurors on the law rather than jurors telling the judges the customary law of the community.

Juries also started to assume their modern role of lie detection.[12] Francis Bacon wrote in 1607 that

> *"the supply of testimony and the discerning and credit of testimony [were left to the] juries consciences and understanding."*

Later in the century Sir Matthew Hale, the legal historian and most distinguished judge of his time, wrote that trial was

> *"the best method of searching and sifting out the truth [because juries] weigh the credibility of Witnesses, and the Force and Efficacy of their Testimonies."*[13]

Thus the old system of relying on oaths as the basis for the criminal justice system was beginning to break down.[14] But this happened slowly, and portions of the old practices remained. By the beginning of the seventeenth century, for example, a defendant still could not subpoena witnesses and, even if the witnesses came to court, they could not testify under oath.[15]

---

8. Barnes at 349–50; Groot, *Prosecutions*, at 141. *See also* Klerman, *Settlement*, at 146, explaining how reforms in criminal law, such as the system of jail delivery or the periodic session of royal justice in the countryside that tried those in jail or on bail, made it more difficult to recruit local jurors. *Id.* at 125, noting that by the fifteenth century jurors did not come from the locality as before.

9. Waldman at 308; Barnes at 350.

10. Klerman, *Settlement*, at 147.

Illustration of the Black Death, from the Toggenburg Bible (1411). The Black Death killed between a third to two-thirds of Europe's population.

11. *See* Theodore Waldman, *Origins of the Legal Doctrine of Reasonable Doubt*, 20 J. Hist. Ideas 299, 314 (1959). *See also generally* Wigmore.

12. Shapiro at 13; Beattie at 235 (citing Shapiro).

13. *Quoted in* Shapiro at 11–12.

14. *See generally* Fisher; Beattie at 235.

Sir Matthew Hale ┆ Sir Francis Bacon

15. Popper at 455–56; Langbein, *Historical Foundations*, at 1055–56 (seventeenth century defendants had no right to compel witness to come to court). *But see* Shapiro at 5–6 (noting Elizabethan legislation allowing for compulsion of witnesses and cross-examination by counsel).

This was in large part to protect from conflicting oaths in court, meaning that someone had committed perjury.

A system that relied on the power of oaths as proof could not suffer even the chance of perjury.

Slowly, though, trial by jury eliminated this problem. The jury's verdict conflicts with nothing because jurors can decide who lied or not.[1] By 1670 trials had advanced to the modern procedure of witnesses offering evidence and jurors making factual conclusions.[2]

All of these developments, however, were still a long way from our Sixth Amendment. The problem for the accused was that the old protections and rough justice of the self-informed jury gave way to a jury ignorant of the parties or dispute. And the process had not become formalized to provide the procedural protections-such as having a right to a lawyer, compulsory process, and confrontation-that the Sixth and Seventh Amendments to the U.S. Constitution guarantee.[3]

But judges were starting to change as well. With more passive jurors there had to be protections to assure the jury only considers valid proofs. These protections are the law of evidence.[4]

EVIDENCE AND THE HEARSAY RULE

With the expanded role of lawyers and the change in the jury from self-informed to ignorant, judges began to regulate the evidence. But evidence law did not start with the new adversarial trials of the nineteenth century. For example, the Romans had rules related to competency, summoning witnesses, privileges, leading questions, corroboration, and authentication of documents.[5]

1. See Fisher at 705–07, noting that the privacy of the jury room hides the shortcomings of the jury system just as the older competency rules hid the shortcomings of the oath system. For critiques of modern jury system and truth, see Oldham, *Truth Telling*, at 118 n.110.

2. Barnes at 356–57 (discussing *Bushell's Case*, Vaughan's Rep. 135 (1670)).

3. See generally Peter Westen, *The Compulsory Process Clause*, 73 Mich. L. Rev. 71 (1974). See **The Sixth Amendment** from this series, Constitution Press, 2017.

4. Fisher at 708; John H. Langbein, *Historical Foundations of the Law of Evidence: A View from the Ryder Sources*, 96 Colum. L. Rev. 1168, 1194 (1996). See also Landsman at 595; Langbein, *Historical Foundations*, at 1170 (no reason for evidence law with the self-informing jury); Morrison at 591, citing 9 Holdsworth, History of English Law 126 (1926) (law of evidence did not grow until sixteenth century when juries were no longer self-informed).

5. See C.A. Morrison, *Some Features of the Roman and the English Law of Evidence*, 33 Tul. L. Rev. 577, 579–81 (1958–59) (for an extensive list). See also Pound at 47–48.

6. Hearsay is "a statement, other than one made by the declarant while testifying at the trial or hearing, offered in evidence to prove the truth of the matter asserted." Fed. R. Evid. 801(a)(c).

7. *Exodus* 20:16; see also *Deuteronomy* 5:20: "Neither shall you bear false witness against your neighbor."

8. Frank R. Herrmann, S.J., *The Establishment of a Rule against Hearsay in Romano-Canonical Procedure*, 36 Va. J. Int'l L. 1, n.285 (1995).

9. Herrmann at 17–18; Morrison at 587.
      The Justinian Code, the *Corpus Juris Civilis* ("Body of Civil Law"), is the modern name for a collection of laws and written procedures from 529 to 534 AD under Justinian I, Byzantine Emperor. See also Wigmore at 437 (focusing on the Germanic and Anglos-Saxon roots of the hearsay rule). But see Morrison at 590 (noting that Wigmore "more often than not" writes of the Roman law of evidence).

Moses with the Ten Commandments by Rembrandt (1659)

Emperor Justinian I

The ancients also had an early hearsay rule.[6]

Ancient Jewish law, for instance, interpreted the Eighth (or Ninth) Commandment that

> "[t]hou shalt not bear false witness against thy neighbor"[7]

as a hearsay rule.[8] The reason was that one who bases his testimony on what others said is a false witness.

Ancient Roman law also had a highly developed hearsay rule. The courts of Cicero's day distrusted *testimonium ex auditu* ("testimony from hearing"). In the later Roman/ Byzantium period, the Justinian Code incorporated the same rule and generally excluded *ex auditu* testimony.[9]

Much of Roman law and the Justinian Code passed into the law of the Catholic Church. Saint Augustine cautioned that only eyewitness testimony was valid.[10] He used the biblical example of the soldiers guarding Christ's tomb. The Pharisees wanted to bribe the soldiers into saying that when they were asleep the Disciples took Christ's body. This would have been hearsay, according to Augustine, because if the soldiers were asleep, how could they see anything?[11]

Pope Gregory the Great was very concerned about defining the elements of a fair trial. Judges, according to Gregory, were to consider only live testimony under oath by witnesses with direct knowledge of the facts. Any reliance on hearsay, *testimonium ex auditu*, was not good judging.[12]

From the church, the hearsay rule passed into the *ius commune* and medieval law. Cases could move forward on the belief of the community or common fame ("*fama*"). But this was only sufficient to begin investigations.[13]

10. Hermmann at 30.

Saint Augustine

11. *Christ Risen from the Tomb* by Piero della Francesca.

Pope Gregory I, known as Gregory the Great

12. Herrmann at 21– 26.　　**13.** Herrmann at 27–29, 47.

From there, the inquest court had to produce actual witnesses who could testify to matters within their direct knowledge.

In the early days of the English common-law jury trial, a hearsay rule would not have made sense. The jurors were self-informed. They would have known who said what before the case went to court.[1] Because the jurors were the witnesses as well, a hearsay rule limiting witness testimony would have been inconsistent with the trial process.

As time when on, though, this began to change. In England the Constitutions of Clarendon of 1164 specified that *"laymen are not to be accused save by proper and legal accusers and witnesses in the presence of the bishop."*[2] The reference to the bishop shows the direct source of the hearsay rule from canon law, which originated in old Roman law.

By the 1600s English courts started to exclude hearsay when the statement stood alone. It could, however, corroborate other testimony.[3] By the beginning of the 1700s, however, the rule against hearsay had become a fundamental principle of the common law.[4]

Much of the hearsay rule's growth in the common law came about because of the old reliance on the power of oaths as the basis for legitimizing the system. Today hearsay is not good evidence because it is not subject to cross-examination and violates the Sixth Amendment's Confrontation Clause. But for the lawyers and judges of the seventeenth and eighteenth centuries, hearsay was not reliable evidence because it was not under oath.[5]

The jury's role had changed. Rather than being self-informed, seventeenth century jurors came to

---

1. *See* Robert Popper, *History and Development of the Accused's Right to Testify*, 1962 Wash. U. L.Q. 454, 455 (1962) (noting jurors were the witnesses).

2. *Quoted in* Leonard W. Levy, Origins of the Fifth Amendment: The Right against Self-Incrimination 45 (1969).

3. Wigmore at 443.   **4.** Wigmore at 458.

5. For Baron Jeffrey Gilbert's evidence treatise, The Law of Evidence (1754), the importance of the oath as basis for hearsay rule rather than lack of cross-examination, see Langbein, *Historical Foundations*, at 1173–76, 1194; Landsman 592.

6. Waldman at 314.

7. William Blake's stylized Isaac Newton illustrates the Age of Reason, with an intellectual giant using his instruments and brain to pierce the darkness.

Newton by William Blake (1805)

8. Wigmore's famous statement is that cross-examination "*is beyond any doubt the greatest legal engine ever invented for the discovery of truth.*" Quoted in Langbein, *Historical Foundations*, at n.32, who argues that "*cross-examination in the hands of a skilled and determined advocate is often an engine of oppression and obfuscation, deliberately employed to defeat the truth.*" On cross-examination and lawyers as the basis for system legitimacy, *see id.* at 1197–98. For cross-examination replacing the oath as guarantor of truth, *see* Wigmore at 448. For more on hearsay in the eighteenth century, *see* Langbein, *Before the Lawyers*, at 301.

9. See *The Sixth Amendment* from this series, **Constitution Press, 2017** (regarding the recognition of the right to a lawyer).

For how the growth of cross-examination brings about the need for trained counsel, see Wigmore at 458 and Landsman at 569–72.

10. Mark DeWolfe Howe, *Juries as Judges of Criminal Law*, 52 Harv. L. Rev. 582, 583 (1938–39). *See generally* Klingelsmith at 107.   Morano at 509 notes that the unchangeable nature of a jury verdict is because it replaced ordeals and the equally unchangeable *Iusticium Dei.*

court to listen and decide the facts before them.[6] Evidence law, based on rational principles, now determined what the jury heard and the parameters of its decision. Thus the trial became like a closed Newtonian system where human reason could discern God's clockwork and find truth.[7]

Now the trained lawyer's cross-examination became the guarantor of truth and the basis for the system's legitimacy, not oaths.[8] But this guarantee assumes both the presence of trained lawyers and a system of procedure that gives them the freedom to exercise their skill.[9]

The early modern jury was only just beginning to see the changes in the system to allow many of the procedural rights we take for granted.

THE EARLY MODERN JURY

After the execution of King Charles I, Parliament abolished the Star Chamber and High Commission courts in 1641. Common-law courts and juries assumed the jurisdiction of these courts.

Jurors from the earliest times had the power of a general verdict, that is, they could declare someone guilty or not guilty without further explanation.[10] This raised the possibility of jury nullification: the jury could protect an accused from the king, reject a bad criminal law, or just give mercy to a guilty but worthy defendant.[11]

If jurors showed too much mercy, however, they ran the risk of imprisonment and fines.[12] Jurors were confined *"without meat, drink, fire or candle"* until they had a verdict.[13] Judges could also influence juries by telling them not only what they thought of the evidence but how the jurors should vote.

---

11. Fisher at 602 and n.83, *citing* THOMAS ANDREW GREEN, VERDICT ACCORDING TO CONSCIENCE: PERSPECTIVES ON THE ENGLISH CRIMINAL TRIAL JURY, 1200–1800, at 28–64 (1985) (noting that medieval law did not provide for manslaughter, and juries would often twist facts to support a self-defense verdict); John H. Langbein, *Shaping the Eighteenth-Century Criminal Trial: A View from the Ryder Sources,* 50 U. CHI. L. REV. 1, 52–55 (1983) (noting nineteenth century jury nullification to temper overly severe laws).

  Later commentators connected this medieval history of jury power and *Magna Carta* to modern justifications of nullification. *See, e.g.,* Steve J. Shone, *Lysander Spooner, Jury Nullification, and Magna Carta,* 22 Q. L. REV. 651, 658–59, 664–65, 666 (2004).

12. The Statute of Winchester of 1285 provided that the king could indict jurors for negligence or concealment of felonies. In 1528, the crown sent jurors that refused to indict in a case with *"pregnant and manifest"* evidence to Fleet Prison. A new jury indicted the defendant. J.G. BELLAMY, THE CRIMINAL TRIAL IN LATER MEDIEVAL ENGLAND 33 (1998). Regarding courts rejecting acquittals, see Langbein, *Before the Lawyers,* at 295.

---

13. BAKER at 75, reporting that in Tudor times the court would fine a juror for eating sweets. This practice continued into the nineteenth century. *See, e.g.,* Glazebrook at 588 (jury sanctions in the context of Throckmorton's trial).

  Again, the movie 12 ANGRY MEN creates dynamic tension by having the jurors locked up together.

  Modern American courts deal with deadlocked jurors with an "Allen charge," an additional instruction to motivate the jury to reach a verdict. The instruction gets it name from *Allen v. United States,* 164 U.S. 492, 501–02 (1896), where the Supreme Court upheld a supplemental instruction given to a deadlocked jury that urged jurors to reconsider their opinions and continue deliberating. *See also United States v. Wills,* 88 F.3d 704, 716 n.6 (9th Cir. 1996) (reviewing circuit case law on *Allen* instructions).

Later courts could also call a second jury, called a "jury of attaint," to review the first jury to decide whether it had willfully falsified its verdict and thus committed perjury. Penalties could include fines, forfeiture of goods, chattels, or lands to the king, and eviction of the jurors' wives and children from their homes.[1]

But it appears that after the overthrow of King Charles I, juries were getting more independent, which John Lilburne's 1649 treason trial shows.

LILBURNE'S JURY

As we have seen, John Lilburne's life was a trial. His 1637 sedition trial and 1649 treason trial were important to the history of the Fifth Amendment and a basis for most of the trial guarantees of the Sixth Amendment.

The record of his trial also informs us about the jury practice of his day.

In his 1649 trial, Lilburne had only two things going for him—the jury and a big mouth:

> "[U]nto the jury, my countrymen, upon whose consciences, integrity and honesty, my life, and the lives and liberties of the honest men of this nation, now lies; who are in law judges of law as well as fact, and you only the pronouncers of their sentence . . . ."[2]

For Lilburne, everything was for the jury's ear.[3] And he could not resist challenging authority, whether king or Cromwell, judge or prosecutor, he made them all look bad:

> "Sir, I entreat you give me leave to read the words of

the law, then; for to the jury I apply, as my judges, both in the law and fact."[4]

In response, one of Lilburne's judges, Jermin, tried lecturing the jury:

> "Let all the hearers know, the jury ought to take notice of it. That the judges that are sworn . . . have ever been the judges of the law . . . and the jury are only judges, whether such a thing were done or no; they are only judges of matter of fact."

After further baiting from Lilburne, Jermin continued:

> "That the jury are the judges of the law, which is enough to destroy all the law in the land; there was never such damnably heresy broached in this nation before."[5]

1. Eric G. Barber, *Judicial Discretion, Sentencing Guidelines, and Lessons from Medieval England*, 1066–1215, 27 W. New Eng. L. Rev. 1, 34 (2008).

2. *Quoted in* Wolfram at 246. For a briefer account of Lilburne's trials as the origins of the American jury rights, see Bachmann at 251–53 and Albert W. Alschuler & Andrew G. Deiss, *A Brief History of the Criminal Jury in the United States*, 61 U. Chi. L. Rev. 867, 902–03 (1994).

3. Wolfram at 251. For other background on the Lilburne trial, see Scott at 397–402. For Lilburne asserting confrontation rights, see Kenneth Graham, *Confrontation Stories: Raleigh on the Mayflower*, 3 Ohio St. J. Crim. L. 209, 212–14 (2005).

4. Wolfram at 246. Regarding Lilburne's self-training in law, see Diane Parkin-Speer, *John Lilburne: A Revolutionary Interprets Statutes and Common Law Due Process*, 1 Law & Hist. Rev. 276 (1983). As we have seen, Lilburne's argument about the tradition of juries defining the law has historical support. Lilburne expounded these ideas in this tract *The Legal Fundamental Liberties of the People of England* (1649). In many ways, Lilburne used his trial of 1649 as the oral presentation of *Fundamental Liberties*.

John Lilburne, known as Freeborn John

Lilburne's jurors must have enjoyed the show. They had sat all day with no break or meal. Just before deliberation, a juror asked for a drink:

"[O]ne of the Jury desired to drink a cup of sack [wine], for they had sat long, and how much longer the debate of the business might last, he knew not; and therefore desired, that they might have amongst them a quart of sack to refresh them."[6]

Despite the long day, the judge denied the juror's request:

"Gentlemen of the jury, I know, for my part, in ordinary juries that they have been permitted to drink before they went from the bar; but in case of Felony or Treason, I never so much as heard it so, or so much as asked for; and therefore you cannot have it."

The judge did, however, allow that the jury "shall have a light" rather than deliberate in the dark.

The jury responded by taking less than two hours to acquit Lilburne.[7] The verdict was met with

"a loud and unanimous shout . . . which lasted for about half an hour without intermission . . . . [An] infinitely enraged and perplexed Cromwell . . . looked upon it as a greater defeat than the loss of a battle would have been."[8]

Lilburne's trial shows a growing tradition of jury independence, which we inherited in the Sixth and Seventh Amendments. But it would be twenty years

before jurors had explicit protection from reprisal for acquitting a defendant.

BUSHELL'S CASE

The power of a judge to punish jurors continued until *Bushell's Case* in 1670, involving William Penn.[9]

Edward Bushell was a juror. In August 1670, he was on the jury that acquitted the Quaker William Penn and William Mead on a charge of unlawful assembly.[10] The judge ordered the jury "*shall not be dismissed until we have a verdict that the court will accept.*" Furthermore, the judge denied the jury food, drink, fire, tobacco— and even a chamber pot![11]

Despite this, the jury continued for acquittal. The judge would not accept the verdict, and he fined the jurors.

---

5. *Quoted in* Wolfram at 247. Given English history of the prior century with Henry VIII's break with Rome and the Puritan revolution, this statement had to have appeared to the jury exaggerated.

6. *Quoted in* Wolfram at 251.

7. Wolfram at 251.

William Penn

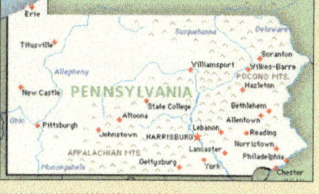

8. Wolfram at 252, *quoting* Lord Clarendon at 4 St. Tr. 1420.

9. William Penn (1644–1718), was the Quaker proprietor of Pennsylvania. His father, Admiral Sir William Penn, a hero of the Dutch War, had high hopes for his son. William disappointed dad by becoming a Quaker. But William, Jr., named Pennsylvania after dad.

10. *See generally* Barnes at 356; SHAPIRO at 13; Kempin at 64; Shone at 654–55; Scott at 394, 406; LOVELL at 407.
   For a modern discussion of jury nullification, see Simon Stern, *Between Local Knowledge and National Politics: Debating Rationales for Jury Nullification after Bushell's Case*, 111 YALE L.J. 1815 (2002).

11. KADRI at 91–92.

Bushell refused to pay. The judge threatened that

"[y]ou shall be locked up without meat, drink, fire, and tobacco. You shall not think thus to abuse the court; we will have a verdict, by the help of God, or you shall starve for it."[1]

Bushell applied for a writ of habeas corpus in the Court of Common Pleas, which held that the trial judge was wrong to override the jury's decision.[2] Lord Chief Justice John Vaughan drew a careful distinction between the respective role of a witness and a juror:

"The Verdict of a Jury, and Evidence of a Witness are very different things . . . A witness swears but to what he hath heard or seen . . . but a jury-man swears to what he can infer and conclude from the testimony of such witnesses by the act and force of his understanding . . . ."[3]

Never again would the law allow a judge to overtly coerce a jury.

The eighteenth century English jury, then, had a lot of discretion.[4] Trials went fast, with *voir dire* to help the defendant choose a jury.[5] The judge did little to instruct the jury, although the judge did contol the evidence and attorneys.[6]

The jurors could ask witnesses questions directly,[7] a throwback to when they were the witnesses, and had free reign to assess a defendant's character.[8] Indeed, by finding defendants guilty of lesser charges, these eighteenth century juries decided punishment.[9]

Despite this power juries became even more separated from their communities. By the early 1700s, juries came from the whole county instead of the local vicinity and had changed from active neighborhood investigators to passive listeners.[10]

---

1. *Quoted in* Levy at 218.

2. Nothing, of course, stops jurors from coercing each other.

3. *Quoted in* Kadri at 91–92.

Chief Justice of the Court of Common Pleas, Sir John Vaughan

4. *See generally* Langbein, *Before the Lawyers*, at 273–77.

5. Langbein, *Before the Lawyers*, at 279. Regarding the speed of eighteenth century English trials, see *id.* at 277–84.

6. Langbein, *Before the Lawyers*, at 284–91. See Langbein, *Historical Foundations*, at 1190 for an account of a judge rejecting the jury's acquittal three times before getting a guilty verdict.

7. Langbein, *Before the Lawyers*, at 288.

8. Langbein, *Before the Lawyers*, at 305.

9. Langbein, *Before the Lawyers*, at 304.

10. Langbein, *Historical Foundations*, at 1170–71.

11. Kadri at 93.

12. See Landsman at 592; Sward, *Civil Trial*, at 370–73.

13. See *The First Amendment*, an illustrated history, in this series, published by Constitution Press. For accounts of the Zenger case, *see* Goldstein at 2-9, *Navarro*, 408 F.3d at 1192; Shone at 655; Scott at 408; Alschuler & Deiss at 871–74, 903 (giving a full account of the changing role of the jury in American history, especially how it has moved from a finder of both fact and law to its much more passive role today).

But what about the jury in America?

JURIES IN AMERICA

The colonists brought the jury with them to America.

Twelve years after his jury trial in England, William Penn guaranteed jury trials in Pennsylvania.[11] King James I guaranteed the jury in the Virginia Company Charter of 1606, and the Massachusetts Body of Liberties likewise incorporated trial by jury.[12]

In the colonial experience juries stood against the crown to protect the colonists' rights. In the case of John Peter Zenger, for instance, a jury of twelve New York colonists acquitted the publisher despite the crown's evidence.[13]

In the Boston writs cases, juries refused to find for the crown.[14] For this reason, the British moved cases involving forfeiture to admiralty courts, without juries.

Thus one of the bases for the American Revolution was King George taking away the jury, as noted in the Declaration of Independence:

"For depriving us, in many cases, of the benefits of Trial by Jury."

The Founders like Thomas Jefferson knew this:

"I consider trial by jury as the only anchor ever yet imagined by man, by which government can be held to the principles of its constitution."[15]

John Adams, often at odds with Jefferson on many ideological points, could not have agreed more:

"It would be an absurdity for jurors to be required to accept the judges' view of the law against their own opinion, judgment, and conscience."[16]

---

14. See *The Third & Fourth Amendments*, in this series, Constitution Press, 2017. *See also* Nelson B. Lasson, The History and Development of the Fourth Amendment of the United States Constitution 51–78 (1937).

15. *Quoted in* Donald M. Middlebrooks, *Reviving Thomas Jefferson's Jury: Sparf and Hansen v. United States Reconsidered*, 46 Am. J. Legal Hist. 353, 353–54 (2004).

Jefferson *also wrote that:* "Were I called upon to decide, whether the people had best be omitted in the legislative or judiciary department, I would say it is better to leave them out of the legislative. The execution of the laws is more important than the making of them." *Id.* See Howe at 582; Alschuler & Deiss at 876–77. *See also* Daniel D. Blinka, *Jefferson and Juries: The Problem of Law, Reason, and Politics in the New Republic*, 47 Am. J. Legal Hist. 35 (2005).

In his *Notes on Virginia*, Jefferson touched on the relationship between jury and judge:
"[I]t is usual for the jurors to decide the fact, and to refer the law arising on it to the judges. But this division of the subject lies with their discretion only. And if the question relate to any point of public liberty, or if it be one of those in which the judges may be suspect of bias, the jury [may] undertake to decide both law and fact."

Thomas Jefferson, Notes on the State of Virginia 140 (J.W. Randolph ed., 1853), *quoted in* Ian Ayres, *Pregnant with Embarrassments: An Incomplete Theory of the Seventh Amendment*, 26 Val. U. L. Rev. 385, 400 (1992). For more on the fact and law dichotomy in the jury and judge relationship, see Ellen E. Sward, *The Seventh Amendment and the Alchemy of Fact and Law*, 33 Seton Hall L. Rev. 573 (2003).

16. *Quoted in* Kempin at 69; Alschuler & Deiss at 906. **Adams** also wrote:
"It is not only his [the juror's] right, but his duty, in that case to find the verdict according to his own best understanding, judgment, and conscience, though in direct opposition to the direction of the court. ... The English law obliges no man ... to put his faith on the sleeve of any mere man." *Quoted in* Howe at 605.

For these men, juries were the bulwark against the tyranny of government.[1] As such, juries had a role in defining and judging the law.[2] In fact, at the time most judges were laymen, not trained lawyers, and comparable to modern justices of the peace.[3]

Thus a colonial jury would have been in as good a position to decide the law as most judges.[4]

Although in colonial America and England jurors had lost their role as self-informed witnesses, they still

decided a defendant's sentence. Statutes existed that defined punishments, but the jurors knew the punishments and could deliberately find a defendant guilty of a lesser offense, despite clear evidence, to avoid the graver punishment.[5]

As in England, many trials

1. Barnes at 362–63. The debates on the Constitution's ratification discussed this issue; see THE FEDERALIST No. 83 as well as ANTI-FEDERALIST No. 83, both of which treat the issue of trial by jury. See also LEVY at 229–30; Barnes at 364; Navarro, 408 F.3d at 1193. Regarding the connection for the Framers between trial by jury and early American democracy, as well as an outline of various early state constitutional protections, see Paul D. Carrington, *The Civil Jury and American Democracy,* 13 DUKE J. COMP. & INT'L L. 79 (2003).

2. Howe at 586. On juries deciding both law and fact, see Barnes at 363–64. For the practice in state courts, see Howe at 595, 601.

3. Howe at 591.

4. In Rhode Island, for example, judges held office "*not for the purpose of deciding causes, for the jury decided all questions of law and fact; but merely to preserve order, and see that the parties had a fair chance with the jury.*" Howe at 590–91.

5. On the jury's role in sentencing in England, see Langbein, *Before the Lawyers,* at 304 (also outlining early plea bargaining); BAKER at 517 (on jury mitigation and the so-called "*pious perjury*" of jury practice). Most crimes in England, many of which we would call minor, were punishable by death, making jury intervention more important. GREEN at 365.
   In 1717, Parliament made many offenses "*clergyable,*" which meant a defendant could receive the common-law version of the medieval church's "*benefit of clergy.*" Chris Kemmitt, *Function over Form: Reviving the Criminal Jury's Historical Role as a Sentencing Body,* 40 U. MICH. J.L. REFORM 93, 98–100 (2006) (a persuasive historical study on the role of original American juries as deciders of the sentence, and recommending that courts should advise modern juries of sentencing consequences to conform to the Framers' original intent). See also Langbein, *Ryder Sources,* at 40–41 (noting the example of finding the defendant guilty of a "clergyable" offense); KIRALFY at 368.

6. John Jay, the first chief justice of the Supreme Court, in a jury trial under the Supreme Court's original jurisdiction, instructed that the jury could judge both facts and law:
   "*It may not be amiss here, gentlemen, to remind you of the good old rule, that on questions of fact it is the province of the jury, on questions of law, it is the province of the court to decide. But it must be observed that by the same law, which recognized this reasonable distribution of jurisdiction, you have nevertheless a right to take upon yourselves to judge of both, and to determine the law as well as the fact in controversy.*" *Georgia v. Brailsford,* 3 U.S. (3 Dall.) at 4 (1794). Discussed in Alschuler & Deiss at 907.

John Jay

were basically sentencing hearings.

As Jefferson's and Adam's views show, the Founders viewed the jury as a bulwark against government oppression. They adopted the general verdict formula, allowing the jury to decide both the law and the facts.[6] A jury in the new U.S. republic was not just a "finder" of fact and law. Rather, the Founders considered the jury to be a mini-legislature.[7]

Alexis de Tocqueville observed that the jury was "*first and foremost a political institution*" and "*a form of popular sovereignty.*"[8] De Tocqueville went on;

"*[t]he jury is both the most effective way of establishing the people's rule and the most efficient way of teaching them how to rule.*"[9]

Samuel Chase

The impeachment of Justice Samuel Chase underscores the importance to the Framers of the idea that the jury should decide the law. One of the charges against Chase was that when sitting as a trial judge he tried "*to wrest from the jury their indisputable right to hear argument, and determine upon the question of law, as well as on the question of fact, involved in the verdict they are required to give.*" Quoted in Alschuler & Deiss at 908. On this and other counts, most senators, though not the two-thirds needed, voted to convict him after the House had impeached him. *Id*.

Although the Chase case was a great win for judicial independence in the new republic, it also shows that, for the Framers, juries deciding the law *was* the law. See WILLIAM H. REHNQUIST, GRAND INQUESTS: THE HISTORIC IMPEACHMENTS OF JUSTICE SAMUEL CHASE AND PRESIDENT ANDREW JOHNSON 595 (1992); Howe, at 588 n.20. For the Chase case and the relationship of judges and juries, see Landsman at 603–04.

de Tocqueville

7. Kemmitt at 103–04. The Framers looked to Aristotle for their ideal of a jury and its role. Equity demands that a jury must be a petit legislature. Aristotle understood that universal law is necessarily overbroad. To prevent injustice a jury or judge must act as the legislature would act if it dealt with this particular case. See Kemmitt at n.99, *citing* ARISTOTLE, ETHICA NICHOMACHEA, *reprinted in* 9 THE WORKS OF ARISTOTLE TRANSLATED INTO ENGLISH 1136–37 (W.D. Ross trans., Clarendon Press 1925). Another systemic manifestation of the exercise of equity was the much broader executive pardoning power in eighteenth century England and America.

8. Kemmitt at 104, *citing* ALEXIS DE TOCQUEVILLE, DEMOCRACY IN AMERICA 313 (Arthur Goldhammer trans., Library of America 2004) (1835). De Tocqueville also described the jury as a "*gratuitous public school, ever open.*" Quoted in Carrington at 86. See also Landsman at 604–05; Aschuler & Deiss at 876.

9. *Quoted in* WILTSHIRE at 165 (*citing* ALEXIS DE TOCQUEVILLE, "*Trial by Jury in the United States Considered as a Political Institution,*" in DEMOCRACY IN AMERICA).

A tension existed in the early republic between the juries deciding law and the emergence of professional judges with an interest in orderly supervision of public affairs.[1] This tension plays out today in debates on jury nullification.

The question is not if the jury has the power to nullify a law or its application; *Bushell's Case* determined that affirmatively in 1670. Rather, the only question is whether the judge should tell jurors of their power and whether lawyers can argue it.[2]

The Supreme Court in 1895 determined this question against informing the jury about jury nullification.[3] The Supreme Court ignored Jefferson and Adams, who expressed the sense of the Founders regarding the jury's proper role.[4] Judges today specifically

1. Howe at 615; *see generally* Shone.

2. Howe at 584. *See* Andrew J. Parmenter, *Nullifying the Jury: "The Judicial Oligarchy" Declares War on Jury Nullification*, 46 WASHBURN L.J. 379 (2007) (discussing the history of jury nullification, including the Lilburne and Bushell trials, up to the modern debate).

Trial by Jury, or Laying Down the Law by Sir Edwin Landseer

The Jury by John Morgan (1861)

This English jury would have known its nullification power and in a system where most crimes were capital, with no plea bargaining, would have regularly exercised it.

For a satirical look at trial by jury in 1840 England, see *Trial by Jury, or Laying Down the Law*, with a French poodle as judge.

4. *But see* Stanton D. Krauss, *An Inquiry into the Right of Criminal Juries to Determine the Law in Colonial America*, 89 J. CRIM. L. & CRIMINOLOGY 111, 122, 214 (1998) (arguing there is not any real evidence that colonial juries had the nullification right).

3. *Sparf and Hansen v. United States*, 156 U.S. 51 (1895). For discussions of *Sparf*, see Howe at 588–89; Shone at 657; Alschuler & Deiss at 910–11; Middlebrooks *generally*.

Modern courts such as the Second Circuit explain that "*the power of juries to 'nullify'. . . is just that—a power; it is by no means a right . . . .*" *United States v. Thomas*, 116 F.3d 606, 615 (2d Cir. 1997). The District of Columbia Circuit Court of Appeals denounces jury nullification even more emphatically: "*A jury has no more 'right' to find a 'guilty' defendant 'not guilty' than it has to find a 'not guilty' defendant 'guilty,' and the fact that the former cannot be corrected by*

a court, while the latter can be, does not create a right out of the power to misapply the law. Such verdicts are lawless, a denial of due process and constitute an exercise of erroneously seized power." *United States v. Washington*, 705 F.2d 489, 494 (D.C. Cir. 1983).

Despite this, the Supreme Court continues to articulate that the jury's very purpose is to prevent government oppression. *See, e.g., United States v. Powell*, 469 U.S. 57, 65 (1984); *Williams v. Florida*, 399 U.S. 78, 100 (1970); *Duncan v. Louisiana*, 391 U.S. 145, 155 (1968) ("*the jury's historic function, in criminal trials, as a check against arbitrary or*

oppressive exercises of power by the Executive Branch"). The function of checking an arbitrary or oppressive power means jury nullification is not only a right but a duty. As Justice Oliver Wendell Holmes wrote: "*The jury has the power to bring in a verdict in the teeth of both law and facts.*" *Horning v. District of Columbia*, 249 U.S. 596 (1920).

For a thoughtful, and thought-provoking, discussion of instructions to modern criminal juries, see B. Michael Dann, *"Must Find the Defendant Guilty": Jury Instructions Violate the Sixth Amendment*, 91 JUDICATURE 12 (2007).

order modern jurors not to consider punishment. This is but one indication that our courts and government have not stayed true to the intent of the Framers and their beliefs on the jury's role.[5]

But despite this, the right to trial by jury is still alive.[6] Today we argue about the details of the right and, though important, even critical, the debate is not fundamental. No one questions a defendant's right to counsel, to compel witnesses, to confront an accuser, to testify under oath, to cross-exam, or to an open trial. Even in civil cases the Seventh Amendment is where the discussion starts.[7]

"By God!," you could exclaim, trial by jury has come a long way.

One of the modern arguments against jury nullification is what happened when Southern juries failed to convict whites accused of killing blacks during the Jim Crow era. *See* James Forman, Jr., *Juries and Race in the Nineteenth Century*, 113 Yale L.J. 895 (2004) (including an interesting outline of how race affected jury composition for most of American history). *See also Navarro*, 408 F.3d at 1194. The modern case of *Batson v. Kentucky*, 476 U.S. 79 (1986), affects jury composition to prevent exclusion of racial minorities from the jury. Even in the Middle Ages a defendant could disqualify a juror for having *"deadly enmities"* or *"greedy desire to get . . . land."* Klerman, *Settlement*, at 134; Levy at 216; Baker at 509.

5. The Queen of Hearts in Lewis Carroll's *Alice's Adventures in Wonderland* (1865) took away all chance for jury nullification. During the trial of the Knave of Hearts, when the King said the jurors should consider the verdict, the Queen declared: *"Sentence first, verdict afterwards."* Kadri at 35.

7. The Seventh Amendment states that it applies *"[i]n suits at common law."* Much modern debate interprets *"the common law"* of 1798 and 1791 to justify limiting the right to a jury. For example, when a federal judge exercises the powers of the old English Chancery courts in "suits in equity," there is no right to a jury. *See* Carrington at 84–85 (noting that the distinction *"is in [most] respects anachronistic because law and equity are seldom distinguished for any other purpose"*). For an insightful comparison of the power of 1791 common-law judges with modern federal judges' powers to deny a litigant the right to a jury through modern procedural devices, *see* Suja A. Thomas, *The Seventh Amendment, Modern Procedure, and the English Common Law*, 82 Wash. U. L.Q. 687 (2004). Thomas well demonstrates that modern judges exercise far greater powers to deny a jury trial than their common-law predecessors. *See also* Paul F. Kirgis, *The Right to a Jury Decision on Questions of Fact under the Seventh Amendment*, 64 Ohio St. L.J. 1125 (2003).

For a contrary view, *see* Edith Guild Henderson, *The Background of the Seventh Amendment*, 80 Harv. L. Rev. 289 (1967) (arguing that colonial jury practice was variable and thus the Seventh Amendment did not intend to codify any specific practice). For a brief discussion of the range of colonial jury and trial practice, *see* Sward, *Civil Trial*, at 369–73, specifically noting that *"[e]quity was a hodgepodge, handled in many different ways, but often by the regular courts of the colonies using procedures drawn for English equity." Id.* at 373.

Regarding problems with the Seventh Amendment's language and grammatically flawed wording, *see* Ayers *generally* and at 386–89.

6. But Is the Jury Vanishing? For concerns, *see* Hon. William G. Young, *Vanishing Trials, Vanishing Juries, Vanishing Constitution*, 40 Suffolk U. L. Rev. 67 (2006); Hon. Sam Sparks & George Butts, *Disappearing Juries and Jury Verdicts*, 39 Tex. Tech. L. Rev. 289 (2007).

BIBLIOGRAPHY

CASES:

Allen v. United States, 164 U.S. 492 (1896).

Apodaca v. Oregon, 406 U.S. 404 (1972).

Ashford v. Thornton, 1 B. & Ald. 405 (1818).

Batson v. Kentucky, 476 U.S. 79 (1986).

Bushell's Case, Vaughan's Reports 135 (1670).

Coffin v. U.S., 156 U.S. 432 (1895).

Duncan v. Louisiana, 391 U.S. 145 (1968).

Georgia v. Brailsford, 3 U.S. (3 Dall.) 4 (1794).

Griffin v. State, 100 Tex. Crim. 641, 274 S.W. 611 (1925).

Horning v. District of Columbia, 249 U.S. 596 (1920).

Ring v. Arizona, 536 U.S. 584 (2002).

Sparf and Hansen v. United States, 156 U.S. 51 (1895).

United States v. Navarro, 408 F.3d 1184 (9th Cir. 2005).

United States v. Powell, 469 U.S. 57 (1984).

United States v. Singer, 380 U.S. 24 (1965).

United States v. Thomas, 116 F. 3d 606 (2d Cir. 1997).

United States v. Washington, 705 F.2d 489 (D.C. Cir. 1983).

United States v. Wills, 88 F.3d 704 (9th Cir. 1996).

Ward v. Commonwealth, 132 Ky. 636, 116 S.W. 786 (1909).

Williams v. Florida, 399 U.S. 78 (1970).

CONSTITUTIONS:

UNITED STATES CONSTITUTION.

THE DECLARATION OF INDEPENDENCE (U.S. 1776).

STATUTES:

Fed. R. Crim. Pro. 23.

Fed. R. Evid. 608.

Fed. R. Evid. 801 (a)(c).

BOOKS:

1 Samuel 17.

A.K.R. KIRALFY, POTTER'S HISTORICAL INTRODUCTION TO ENGLISH LAW, 4TH ED. (1958).

ALEXIS DE TOCQUEVILLE, DEMOCRACY IN AMERICA (Arthur Goldhammer trans., The Library of America 2004) (1835).

ALISON WEIR, QUEEN ISABELLA (2005).

ANTI-FEDERALIST No. 83.

BARBARA J. SHAPIRO, "BEYOND REASONABLE DOUBT" AND "PROBABLE CAUSE" (1991).

BARON JEFFREY GILBERT, THE LAW OF EVIDENCE (1754).

BLACK'S LAW DICTIONARY (5th ed. 1979).

BLACKSTONE, COMMENTARIES ON THE LAWS OF ENGLAND (University of Chicago Press 1979 (1765-69).

BRYCE LYON, A CONSTITUTIONAL AND LEGAL HISTORY OF MEDIEVAL ENGLAND (1960).

COLIN R. LOVELL, ENGLISH CONSTITUTIONAL AND LEGAL HISTORY (1962).

DANIEL J. KORNSTEIN, SHAKESPEAR'S LEGAL APPEAL (1994).

DANNY DANZIGER & JOHN GILLINGHAM, 1215: THE YEAR OF MAGNA CARTA (2003).

DANTE, THE DIVINE COMEDY

Exodus 20:13.

FREDERICK G. KEMPIN, JR., HISTORICAL INTRODUCTION TO ANGLO-AMERICAN LAW (3d ed. 1990).

H.W. FOWLER, A DICTIONARY OF MODERN ENGLISH USAGE (2nd ed. 1965).

G.K. CHESTERTON, TREMENDOUS TRIFLES (1968).

Genesis 18, 20-32.

GEORGE J. EDWARDS, THE GRAND JURY: AN ESSAY (1906).

HOWARD W. GOLDSTEIN, GRAND JURY PRACTICE (2005).

J.G. BELLAMY, THE CRIMINAL TRIAL IN LATER MEDIEVAL ENGLAND (1998).

J. H. BAKER, AN INTRODUCTION TO ENGLISH LEGAL HISTORY (4th ed. 2002).

JOHN AYTO, DICTIONARY OF WORD ORIGINS (1990).

JOHN PHILLIP REID, THE ANCIENT CONSTITUTION AND THE ORIGINS OF ANGLO-AMERICAN LIBERTY (2005).

KURT VON S. KYNELL, SAXON AND MEDIEVAL ANTECEDENTS OF THE ENGLISH COMMON LAW (2000).

Laws of William, c. 6.

LEONARD W. LEVY, ORIGINS OF THE FIFTH AMENDMENT: THE RIGHT AGAINST SELF-INCRIMINA-TION (1969).

LEWIS CARROLL, ALICE'S ADVENTURES IN WONDERLAND (1865).

NELSON B. LASSON, THE HISTORY AND DEVELOPMENT OF THE FOURTH AMENDMENT OF THE UNITED STATES CONSTITUTION (1937).

O.F. ROBINSON, THE CRIMINAL LAW OF ANCIENT ROME (1995).

Peter Earle, *Richard II* in THE LIVES OF THE KINGS AND QUEENS OF ENGLAND (Antonia Fraser ed. 1975).

Proverbs 11:29.

R.C. VAN CAENEGEM, THE BIRTH OF THE ENGLISH COMMON LAW (1988).

ROBERT BALDICK, THE DUEL: A HISTORY (1965).

Roger D. Groot, *The Early Thirteenth Century Criminal Jury*, in TWELVE GOOD MEN AND TRUE: THE CRIMINAL TRIAL JURY IN ENGLAND, 1200-1800 (J.S. Cockburn & Thomas A Green eds., 1988).

ROSCOE POUND, THE LAWYER FROM ANTIQUITY TO MODERN TIMES (1951).

SADAKAT KADRI, THE TRIAL: A HISTORY, FROM SOCRATES TO O.J. SIMPSON (2005).

SEAMUS HEANEY, BEOWULF: A NEW VERSE TRANSLATION 39 (2000).

SIR WALTER SCOTT, IVANHOE (1819).

SUSAN FORD WILTSHIRE, GREECE, ROME, AND THE BILL OF RIGHTS (1992).

THE FEDERALIST No. 83 (Alexander Hamilton).

THE *Placita Corone* (circa 1274–75).

THE WORKS OF ARISTOTLE TRANSLATED INTO ENGLISH (W.D. Ross trans., Clarendon Press 1925).

THE WORKS OF PLATO, *Apology* (Irwin Edman ed., Benjamin Jowett trans., Random House 1956).

THOMAS ANDREW GREEN, VERDICT ACCORDING TO CONSCIENCE: PERSPECTIVES ON THE ENG-
    LISH CRIMINAL TRIAL JURY, 1200–1800 (1985).

THOMAS JEFFERSON, NOTES ON THE STATE OF VIRGINIA (J.W. Randolph ed., 1853).

WALTER ULLMANN, JURISPRUDENCE IN THE MIDDLE AGES (1980).

WEBSTER'S NEW INT'L DICTIONARY (2d ed. 1942).

WILLIAM H. REHNQUIST, GRAND INQUESTS: THE HISTORIC IMPEACHMENTS OF JUSTICE SAMUEL
    CHASE AND PRESIDENT ANDREW JOHNSON (1992).

ARTICLES:

Adriaan Lanni, *"Verdict Most Just": The Modes of Classical Athenian Justice,* 16 YALE J.L. &
    HUMAN. 277 (2004).

Albert W. Alschuler & Andrew G. Deiss, *A Brief History of the Criminal Jury in the United States*,
    61 U. CHI. L. REV. 867 (1994).

Alison L. LaCroix, *To Gain the Whole World and Lose His Own Soul: Ninteenth Centruy American
    Dueling as Public Law and Private Code*, 33 HOFSTRA L. REV. 501 (2004).

Amalia D. Kessler, *Our Inquisitorial Tradition: Equity Procedure, Due Process, And The Search For
    An Alternative To The Adversarial*, 90 CORNELL L. REV. 1181 (2005).

Andrea McKenzie, *"This Death Some Strong and Stout Hearted Man Doth Choose": The Practice of
    Peine Forte Et Dure in Seventeen- and Eighteenth-Century England*, 23 LAW & HIST. REV. 279
    (2005).

Andrew J. Parmenter, *Nullifying the Jury: "The Judicial Oligarchy" Declares War on Jury Nullifica-
    tion*, 46 WASHBURN L. J. 379 (2007).

Anthony Morano, *A Reexamination of the Development of the Reasonable Doubt Rule,* 55 B.U.L.
    REV. 507 (1975).

Anthony Musson, *Twelve Good Men and True? The Character of Early Fourteenth-Century Juries,*
    15 LAW & HIST. REV. 115 (1997).

B. Michael Dann, *"Must Find the Defendant Guilty": Jury Instructions Violate the Sixth Amendment,*
    91 JUDICATURE 12 (2007).

C.A. Morrison, *Some Features of the Roman and the English Law of Evidence*, 33 TUL. L. REV. 577
    (1958-59).

Charles Gross, *The Early History and Influnce of the Office of Coroner,* 7 POLITICAL SCIENCE QUAR-
    TERLY 656 (1892).

Charles H. Haskins, *The Early Norman Jury,* 8 AM. HIST. REV. 613 (1903).

Chris Kemmitt, *Function Over Form: Reviving The Criminal Jury's Historical Role As A Sentencing
    Body*, 40 U. MICH. J.L. REFORM 93 (2006).

Daniel D. Blinka, *Jefferson and Juries: The Problem of Law, Reason, and Politics in the New Republic*,
    47 AM. J. LEGAL HIST. 35 (2005).

David Crook, *Triers and the Origin of the Grand Jury,* 12 J. LEG. HIST. 103 (1991).

Daniel Klerman, *Settlement and the Decline of Private Prosecution in Thirteen-Century England*, 19
    LAW & HIST. REV. 1 (2001).

Daniel Klerman, *Was the Jury Ever Self-Informing?,* 77 S. CAL. L. REV. 123 (2003).

Diane Parkin-Speer, *John Lilburne: a Revolutionary Interprets Statutes and Common Law Due
    Process*, 1 LAW & HIST. REV. 276 (1983).

Donald M. Middlebrooks, *Reviving Thomas Jefferson's Jury: Sparf and Hansen v. United States
    Reconsidered*, 46 AM. J. LEGAL HIST. 353 (2004).

Edith Guild Henderson, *The Background of the Seventh Amendment*, 80 HARV. L. REV. 289 (1967).

Ellen E. Sward, *A History of the Civil Trial in the United States*, 51 U. KAN. L. REV. 347 (2003).

Ellen E. Sward, *The Seventh Amendment and the Alchemy of Fact and Law*, 33 SETON HALL L. REV. 573 (2003).

Eric G. Barber, *Judicial Discretion, Sentencing Guidelines, and Lessons from Medieval England, 1066-1215*, 27 W. NEW ENG. L. REV. 1 (2008).

Ethan J. Leib, *Supermajoritarianism and the American Criminal Jury*, 33 HASTINGS CONST. L.Q. 141 (2006).

Frank R. Herrmann, S.J., *The Establishment of a Rule Against Hearsay in Romano-Canonical Procedure*, 36 VA. J. INT'L L. 1 (1995).

George C. Thomas, III, *History's lesson for the right to counsel*, 2004 U. Ill. L. Rev. 543 (2004).

George Jarvis Thompson, *The Development of the Anglo-American Judicial System: History of the English Court to the Judicature Acts*, 17 CORNELL L.Q. 9, (1931-32).

Harold W. Wolfram, *John Lilburne: Democracy's Pillar of Fire*, 3 SYRACUSE L. REV. 213 (1952).

Helene E. Schwartz, *Demythologizing the Historic Role of the Grand Jury*, 10 AM. CRIM. L. REV. 701 (1972).

Honorable William G. Young, *Vanishing Trials, Vanishing Juries, Vanishing Constitution*, 40 SUF-FOLK U. L. REV. 67 (2006).

Ian Ayres, *Pregnant with Embarrassments: An Incomplete Theory of the Seventh Amendment*, 26 VAL. U. L. REV. 385 (1992).

Irwin Langbein, *The Jury of Presentment and the Coroner*, 33 COLUM. L. REV. 1329 (1933).

Jacob Reynolds, *The Rule Of Law And The Origins Of The Bill Of Attainder Clause*, 18 ST. THOMAS L. REV. 177 (2005).

James B. Thayer, *The Jury and Its Development*, 5 HARV. L. REV. 249 (1891-92).

James B. Thayer, *The Older Modes of Trial*, 5 HARV. L.REV. 45 (1891-92).

James C. Oldham, *The Origins of the Special Jury*, 50 UNIV. CHICAGO L. REV. 137 (1983).

James C. Oldham, *Truth-Telling in the Eighteenth-Century English Courtroom*, 12 LAW & HIST. REV. 95 (1994).

James Forman, Jr. *Juries and Race in the Nineteenth Century*, 113 YALE L.J. 895 (2004).

Jeffrey Omar Usman, *Ancient and Modern Character Evidence: How Character Evidence Was Used in Ancient Athenian Trials, Its Uses in the United States, and What This Means for How These Democratic Societies Understood the Role of Jurors*, 33 OKLA. CITY U.L. REV. 1 (2008).

John F. Decker, *Legislating New Federalism: The Call for Grand Jury Reform in the States*, 58 OKLA. L. REV. 341 (2005).

John W. Baldwin, *The Intellectual Preparation for the Canon of 1215 Against Ordeals*, 36 SPECU-LUM 613 (1961).

John H. Langbein, *Historical Foundations of the Law of Evidence: A View from the Ryder Sources*, 96 COLUM. L. REV. 1168 (1996).

John H. Langbein, *Shaping the Eighteenth-Century Criminal Trial: A View from the Ryder Sources*, 50 U. CHI. L. REV. 1 (1983).

John H. Langbein, *The Criminal Trial Before the Lawyers*, 45 U. CHI. L. REV. 263 (1977-78).

John H. Wigmore, *The History of the Hearsay Rule* 17 HARV. L. REV. 437 (1903-04).

Julian S. Waterman, *Thomas Jefferson and Blackstone's Commentaries*, 27 ILL. L. REV. 629 (1932-33).

Justin C. Barnes, *Lessons Learned from England's "Great Guardian of Liberty": A Comparative Study of English and American Civil Juries*, 3 U. ST. THOMAS L.J. 345 (2005).

Kenneth Graham, *Confrontation Stories: Raleigh on the Mayflower*, 3 Ohio St. J. Crim. L. 209 (2005).

Kevin K. Washburn, *Restoring The Grand Jury*, 76 FORDHAM L. REV. 2333 (2008).

Margaret C. Klingelsmith, *New Readings of Old Law*, 66 U. PA. L. REV. 107 (1917-18).

Margaret H. Kerr, Richard D. Forsyth, and Michael J. Plyley, *Cold Water and Hot Iron: Trial by Ordeal in England*, 22 J. INTERDISCIPLINARY HIST. 573 (1992).

Mark DeWolfe Howe, *Juries as Judges of Criminal Law*, 52 HARV. L. REV. 582 (1938-39).

Matthew P. Harrington, *The Economic Origins of the Seventh Amendment*, 87 IOWA L. REV. 145 (2001).

Michael D. Gordon, *The Perjury Statute of 1563: A Case History of Confusion*, 124 PROCEEDINGS OF THE AM. PHILOSOPHICAL SOCIETY 438 (1980).

Mike MacNair, *Vicinage and the Antecedents of the Jury*, 17 LAW & HIST. REV. 537 (1999).

Morgan, *A Brief History of Special Verdicts and Special Interrogatories* 32 YALE L. J. 575 (1923).

Morris S. Arnold, *Law and Fact in Medieval Jury Trial: Out of Sight, Out of Mind*, 18 AM. J. LEGAL HIST. 267 (1974).

Naomi D. Hurnard, *The Jury of Presentment and the Assize of Clarendon*, 56 ENGLISH HIST. REV. 374 (1941).

Niki Kuckes, *The Democratic Prosecutor: Explaining the Constitutional Function of the Federal Grand Jury*, 94 GEO. L. J. 1265 (2006).

Patrick Wormald, *Neighbors, Courts, and Kings: Reflections on Michael Macnair's Vicini*, 17 LAW & HIST. REV. 597 (1999).

Paul D. Carrington, *The Civil Jury and American Democracy*, 13 DUKE J. COMP. & INT'L L. 79 (2003).

Paul F. Kirgis, *The Right to a Jury Decision on Questions of Fact Under the Seventh Amendment*, 64 OHIO ST. L. J. 1125 (2003).

Paul R. Hyams, *The Charter as a Source for the Early Common Law*, 12 J. LEGAL HIST. 173 (1991).

Peter Brown, *Society and the Supernatural: A Medieval Change*, 104 DAEDALUS 133 (1975).

Peter Westen, *The Compulsory Process Clause*, 73 MICH. L. REV. 71 (1974).

Phillip B. Scott, *Jury Nullification: An Historical Perspective on a Modern Debate*, 91 W. VA. L. REV. 389 (1988).

R.H. Helmholz, *Crime, Compurgation and the Courts of the Medieval Church*, 1 LAW & HIST. Rev. 1 (1983).

R.H. Helmholz, *The Early History of the Grand Jury and the Canon Law*, 50 U. CHI. L. REV. 613 (1983).

Ralph V. Turner, *The Origins of the Medieval Jury: Frankish, English, of Scandinavian?*, 7 J. OF BRITISH STUDIES 1 (1968).

Rebecca V. Colman, *Reason and Unreason in Early Medieval Law*, 4 J. OF INTERDISCIPLINARY HIST. 571 (1974).

Roger A. Fairfax, Jr., *The Jurisdictional Heritage of the Grand Jury Clause*, 91 MINN. L. REV. 398 (2006).

Roger D. Groot, *The Jury in Private Criminal Prosecutions before 1215*, 27 AM. J. LEGAL HIST. 116 (1983).

Roger D. Groot, *The Jury of Presentment Before 1215*, 26 AM. J. LEGAL HIST. 1 (1992).

Simon Stern, *Between Local Knowledge and National Politics: Debating Rationales for Jury Nullification after Bushell's Case*, 111 YALE L. J. 1815 (2002).

Sir Frederick Pollock, *The King's Peace in the Middle Ages*, 13 HARV. L. REV. 177 (1900).

Stanton D. Krauss, *An Inquiry into the Right of Criminal Juries to Determine the Law in Colonial America*, 89 J. Crim. L. & Criminology 111 (1998).

Stephan Landsman, *The Civil Jury in America: Scenes from an Unappreciated History*, 44 Hastings L. J. 579 (1993).

Steve Bachmann, *Starting Again with the Mayflower … England's Civil War and America's Bill of Rights*, 20 QLR 194 (2001).

Steve J. Shone, *Lysander Spooner, Jury Nullification, and Magna Carta*, 22 Q. L. R. 651, 658 (2004).

Suja A. Thomas, *The Seventh Amendment, Modern Procudure, and the English Common Law*, 82 Wash. U. L. Q. 687 (2004).

Theodore Waldman, *Origins of the Legal Doctrine of Reasonable Doubt*, 20 J. of Hist. of Ideas 299 (1959).

Trisha Olson, *Of Enchantment: The Passing of the Ordeals and the Rise of the Jury Trial*, 50 Syracuse L. Rev. 109 (2000).

W.A. Morris, *The Sheriff and the Justices of William Rufus and Henry I*, 7 Cal. L. Rev. 235 (1910).

Walter Ullmann, *Some Medieval Principles of Criminal Procedure*, 59 (LIX) Juridical Rev. 1 (1947).

Movies and Television:

. . . And Justice for All (Columbia Pictures 1979).

12 Angry Men (United Artists 1957).

A Knight's Tale (Colombia Pictures 2001).

Bill & Ted's Excellent Adventure (Orion Pictures 1989).

Camelot (Warner Brothers 1967).

Cheaper by the Dozen (20th Century Fox 2003) and (20th Century Fox 1950).

Cop (1988).

Cop Out (Warner Bros. 2010).

Cops (March 11, 1989 March 21, 2009).

El Cid (Allied Artists 1961).

Excalibur (Warner Brothers 1981).

High Noon (United Artists 1952).

Inherit the Wind (United Artists 1960).

Ivanhoe (MGM 1952).

Law & Order: Trial by Jury (March 3, 2005 - May 6, 2006).

Monty Python and the Holy Grail (1975).

Philadelphia (TriStar Pictures 1993).

Star Wars (20th Century Fox 1977).

The 13th Warrior (Touchstone Pictures 1999).

The Crucible (20th Century Fox 1996).

The Dirty Dozen (MGM 1967).

The Duelists (Paramount Pictures 1977).

The Juror (Sony 1996).

Tombstone (Hollywood Pictures 1993).

Trial by Jury (1875).

Trial by Jury (Morgan Creek 1994).

The Verdict (Warner Bro. 1946).

THE VERDICT (20th Century Fox 1982).

MISCELLANEOUS:

http://www.constitution.org/liberlib.htm (last visited 1 June 2007).

CPSIA information can be obtained
at www.ICGtesting.com
Printed in the USA
BVOW05s1816281117
501485BV00006B/16/P